Keto Meal Prep

> The Complete Keto Meal Prep Guide for Beginners, 28 Days Keto Meal Plan Help You to Lose Weight 20 Pounds, Saving Time and Money

By Denier Cristal

Copyright© 2018 By Danier Cristal

All Right Reserved.

In no way it is legal to reproduce, duplicate, or transmit any part of this document by either electronic means or printed format. Any recording of this publication is strictly prohibited, and any storage of this material is not allowed unless with a written permission from the publisher.

The information provided herein is stated to be truthful, by any usage or abuse of any processes or directions contained in this book is the solitary and complete responsibility of the reader. Under no circumstances, will any legal liability or blame be held against the publisher for any reparation, damages, or monetary loss due to the information herein, either directly or indirectly.

Legal Notice:

This book is copyright protected. You cannot amend, distribute, sell, use, quote or paraphrase any part or the content within this book without the consent of the author. Legal action will be pursued if it is breached

Disclaimer notice:

Please note the information inhere is for educational and enchainment purposes only. Every attempt has been made 10 provide accurate, up to date and reliable, complete information. No warranties of any kind are expressed or implied. Readers acknowledge that the author is not engaging in the rendering of legal, financial, medical or professional advice.

By reading this document, the reader agrees that under no circumstances are we responsible for any losses, direct or indirect, which are incurred as a result of the use of information contained in this document, including but not limited to errors, omissions, or any inaccuracies.

Table of Content

INTRODUCTION 1

PART 1: MY WEIGHT LOSS STORY 2

PART 2. THE BASIC OF MEAL PREP 5

    WHAT IS MEAL PREP? 5
    WHY MEAL PREP? 5
    PREPARATION BEFORE MEAL PREP 7
    THE ART OF STORING ON MEAL PREP 7
    HELPFUL TIPS AND MISTAKES TO AVOID 9
    DIY MEAL PREP FOR YOUR DAILY PLAN 11

PART 3. UNDERSTANDING THE KETOGENIC DIET 13

    WHAT IS THE KETOGENIC DIET 13
    BENEFITS OF KETOGENIC DIET 14
    IS THE KETOGENIC DIET SUITABLE FOR ME? 16
    WHAT TO EAT ON KETO DIET 17
    WHAT NOT TO EAT 18
    COMMON KETO INGREDIENTS FOR MEAL PREP SHOPPING 19

PART 4 MEAL PREP 21

MEAL PREP 1: THE FIRST TWO DAYS ON KETO DIET 22

    BREAKFAST: *COCONUT FLOUR NORTHERN PANCAKES* 24
    BREAKFAST: *EGG STUFFED PORTOBELLO MUSHROOMS* 25
    LUNCH: *GROUND MEAT CASSEROLE* 27
    SOUP: *BROCCOLI SOUP* 28
    SNACK: *GROUND BEEF, CHEESE MEATBALLS* 29
    DINNER: *TUSCAN CHICKEN* 30

MEAL PREP 2: THE 3RD AND 4TH DAYS ON KETO DIET 33

    BREAKFAST: *GLUTEN FREE CEREAL* 35
    BREAKFAST: *MUSHROOM OMELETTE WITH HAM AND CHEESE* 36
    LUNCH: *MUSSELS WITH CREAM AND BACON* 37
    SNACK: *STUFFED PEPPERS* 38
    DINNER: *CHICKEN CURRY* 39
    APPETIZER: *CRAB, AVOCADO AND FENNEL SKILLET* 40

MEAL PREP 3: THE 5TH, 6TH, AND 7TH DAYS ON KETO DIET 42

BREAKFAST: LOW CARB KETOGENIC FRITTATA 44
SALAD: CESAR SALAD WITH BACON AND VINAIGRAITTE 45
LUNCH: GRILLED SALMON WITH AVOCADO 46
LUNCH : BUFFALO CHICKEN WINGS 47
SNACK: STUFFED ZUCCHINI 48
DINNER: ALMOND FLOUR BURGER WITH GOAT CHEESE 49

MEAL PREP 4: THE 8TH AND 9TH DAY OF THE KETO DIET 51

BREAKFAST: KETOGENIC BISCUITS WITH CHEESE SAUCE 53
BREAKFAST: RASPBERRY BREAKFAST BOWLS 54
LUNCH: ASIAN STYLE BEEF ZOODLES 55
SOUP: LEEK AND SALMON SOUP 56
SNACK: BROCCOLI CHEESE BALLS 57
DINNER: SAUSAGE SKILLET WITH CABBAGE 58

MEAL PREP 5: THE 10TH AND 11TH DAYS ON KETO DIET 60

BREAKFAST: LOW CARB, KETOGENIC WAFFLES 62
BREAKFAST: CHIA PUDDING 63
LUNCH: SHRIMP AND BROCCOLI PAELLA 64
SOUP: VEGETABLE SOUP 66
SNACK: DEVILED EGGS 67
DINNER : CHICKEN AND BROCCOLI GRATIN 68

MEAL PREP 6: THE 12TH; 13TH AND 14TH DAY ON KETO DIET 70

BREAKFAST: VANILLA AND CHIA SMOOTHIE 72
BREAKFAST: PEACH COBBLER 73
LUNCH: LETTUCE WRAPS WITH BACON 74
SOUP: BROCCOLI AND YOGURT SOUP 75
SNACK: SAUSAGE DIP 77
DINNER: CHICKEN PIZAIOLA 78

MEAL PREP 7: THE 15TH AND 16TH DAYS ON KETO DIET 81

BREAKFAST: GRANOLA BARS 83
APPETIZER: STUFFED CUCUMBERS 84
LUNCH : SALMON WITH CAPERS 85
LUNCH : TURKEY CURRY 86
SALAD : SALMON AND AVOCADO SALAD 87
DINNER : CAULIFLOWER PIZZA 88

MEAL PREP 8: THE 17TH AND 18TH DAYS ON KETO DIET 90

- BREAKFAST: Cocoa chocolate shake 92
- LUNCH : Chuck roast with balsamic vinegar 93
- STEW :Spinach and onion stew 95
- SNACK :Stuffed tomatoes 96
- DINNER: Ketogenic low carb Cloud Bread 97
- DINNER : Ketogenic Bruschetta 98

MEAL PREP 9: THE 19TH, 20TH AND 21ST DAYS ON KETO DIET 100

- BREAKFAST :Liver and beef patties with eggs 102
- APPETIZER : Cauliflower fritters 103
- LUNCH: Ketogenic Sushi 104
- LUNCH :Pork chops with apples 105
- SNACK :Pineapples with bacon 106
- SALAD : Salmon salad with red onions and granny smith apples 107

MEAL PREP 10: THE 22ND AND 23RD DAYS ON KETO DIET 109

- BREAKFAST : Avocado, almond milk smoothie 111
- LUNCH : Eggplant sandwiches 112
- SNACK : Scottish eggs 113
- DINNER : Ahi tuna bowl 114
- DINNER: Stuffed Spinach and beef burgers 115
- SALAD : Shrimp Salad 117

MEAL PREP 11:THE 24TH AND 25TH DAYS ON KETO DIET 119

- BREAKFAST: Almond flour Bread 121
- APPETIZER : Salmon rolls with cucumber 122
- LUNCH : Ketogenic chicken skillet 123
- DINNER :Instant Pot Ketogenic Chili 125
- SNACK : Instant Pot Stuffed olives 126
- SALAD :Instant Pot Tuna Salad 128

MEAL PREP 12: THE 26TH, 27TH AND 28TH DAYS ON KETO DIET 131

- BREAKFAST: Egg cups with sausage crumbles 133
- APPETIZER: Chicken wings 134
- LUNCH: Tandoori Chicken 135
- LUNCH: Shrimp Scampi 137
- SNACK : Instant Pot Kale Chips 138
- DINNER : Steak with broccoli 139

CONCLUSION 140

Introduction

Let me start this Keto Meal Prep Journey by thanking you and expressing my gratitude for you for choosing this book amongst many to read. I can't find enough words to express how grateful I am for having you read this book and the huge appreciation I feel for the time you have spent in picking this book to purchase, download and read my book.

By writing this book and offering it to you, my core aim is to share you with my large experience in keto meal prep to help to lose weight, save your time and money. Through this keto recipe meal Prep cookbook, I ensure that all of you, dear readers can be easy to grasp the concept of Meal Prep combined with the Keto diet. My centre of interest was only your health and your well being.

I am very excited to share with you this highly-effective, yet simple keto meal prep cookbook that will revolutionize your culinary traditions and your life in general. And I hope, through this recipe meal prep cookbook, to pass my knowledge and my passion for healthy food to you. I will try to teach you how to meal prep and plan for your food so that you will be able to discover the joy of the culinary world and its healthy meals. There are several keto meal preps in this cookbook that include about 72 recipes, which I carefully chose from affordable, easy-to find and simple ingredients that you can get from any close grocery.

Each of recipes provides you with the exact measurements for a serving size that goes hand in hand with the number of days you prep meals for. And all of recipes are balanced in calories and will help you maintain your carbohydrate intake under control. I also provide you with the nutrition information of each recipe to help you stay healthy. I make sure to include the cooking time you need and the preparation as well.

And I hope that my recommendations and my recipes help you meal prep your culinary plan in a healthier way. I truly believe you can cook just the way I do if you have the passion for your family and to be healthier.

I wish you have a healthy, happy and easy meal prep cooking journey!

Part 1: My Weight Loss Story

Are you always feeling exhausted of gaining weight even without trying to?
Are you feeling tired and don't know why?

If you feel any of these symptoms, then I should tell you that I know exactly what you are suffering from and how you feel. Because I felt the same feeling and went through the same experience as you.

After the birth of my baby, I spent my most of time on weight loss when my weight gained up to 200 lb. two years ago. I was ashamed of the way I looked in the mirror and always wanted to have a perfect shape.I was afraid of weighing myself on the scale every time. And what's more painful was that my health tarted shambling although I would get enough sleep. I felt my body was deteriorating and I couldn't control my health any more. When I saw people in the weight loss group saying keto diet was good for weight loss, I decided to try the healthy keto diet lifestyle. The Ketogenic diet is not a diet or a trendy health style that will restrict your meals and will torture you by limiting your food meals. After having a month of keto diet, I feel better and better.

When it comes to the Ketogenic diet ,You may meet many people who are skeptical. It may be quiet puzzling that you can lose weight while you can still consume foods that are specifically high in fats. I do get it and I really understand your doubts. I suffered from overweight , ups and downs in my energy levels and my sugar level was unstable most of the times.

It is true that starting the ketogenic diet was a hard struggle for me at first. Especially when I paid attention to food labels, calculated calories and carbohydrates or bother with the nutritional information. But when I realized that my health was at stake, I made my decision to make an upheaving change and keep on this keto diet.

Adopting a keto diet doesn't necessarily mean to cut off all your favourite staples. You don't have to be strict to your health and obsessed with too much exercising.

This diet is mainly based on ketosis, which is a process that makes your body a fat-burning machine. By making all the dietary changes to your daily meal plan, you can empower your body rather from burning carbohydrates to burning fat for more energy.

After a few weeks of making a ketogenic diet swap, I started noticing the huge difference. I was really amazed that my pants became a little bit looser than it used to be. So if you are wondering about the basics of this Ketogenic diet, well, I should tell you that the ketogenic diet is very efficient for your weight loss.

When I knew the meal prep and meal plan combined with keto diet were more efficient and could save my time and money. I did not need to spend time on selecting which keto recipes I should have, and I did not need to calculate the nutrition intake everyday when I made a meal plan with preparation. I was so excited that I could spend more time looking after my little baby and staying with my family.

Part 2. The Basic of Meal Prep

Now I'd like to illustrate some basics of Meal Prep for you.

The ketogenic diet may have A LOT of restrictions in terms of food. But even if this is the case, it is easy to follow—especially if YOU plan ahead. Planning ahead allows you to carefully select the types of food that goes into your plate so that you can keep your body in a constant state of ketosis.

What Is Meal Prep?

So, what is meal prep? It is simply making your meals ahead of time! So, you don't have to cook day in and day out. What you are doing here is essentially preparing your meals ahead of time and storing these pre-cooked meals in containers. Meal prepping is perfect for people—like you and me—who live busy lives yet still want to have full control over the food we eat and the benefits that we get from whole foods.

This practice may occur among people who desire to lose weight or maintain a healthy lifestyle. Advance preparation can serve to standardize food portions. Sometimes meals are fully cooked, other times they are not. Mcals may be prepared in small containers such as tupperware, and are sometimes labeled

Why Meal Prep?

I especially like meal prep! Even studies show that planning can increase your likelihood of following through and achieving your goals. Those who plan ahead—whether it is your workout or meals—are able to succeed. But more than just being successful in our weight loss goals, there is more to meal prep than meets the eye. Read on!

- **You can avoid decision fatigue:** What am I going to eat today? What is there to eat? Are just some of the few questions you need not to ask yourself on a daily basis when on meal prep. One of the reasons why many people lose your motivation on following the ketogenic diet is that you get tired of figuring out which food is acceptable, and which isn't. When you start to experience decision fatigue, you are prone to grabbing any food that you can find in your pantry or fridge. That's why if you plan your meals in advance, you will be able to reduce your choices so that you are not tempted to eat anything else. This frees up your mental space so that you can focus on more important things.

- **Saves you time and energy:** People can't seem to follow the ketogenic diet because you do not have the time and energy to cook your meals at home. But if you do meal prepping, you only need a few hours each week to prepare everything. This saves you time and energy on preparing and figuring out what to eat on a daily basis.

- **Grocery shopping becomes easier:** Planning your meals in advance allows you to know which ingredients you need to buy. You can easily make a list of what you need to buy so that you don't buy other food ingredients not needed for that week of meal prepping.

- **Saves money:** Didn't you know that you can save money with meal prepping? Meal prepping allows you to check your inventory and see if there are ingredients in your fridge that you can use. But more than effectively use your inventory, you can also make a lot of savings if you buy items in bulk.

- **You stay in the state of ketosis effectively:** One of the biggest benefits that you can get from the ketogenic diet is that you will be able to stay in ketosis more effectively. To stay in ketosis, you need to keep track of your macros to make sure that you are eating the right proportion of fats, protein, and carbohydrates. The thing is, meal prepping allows you to calculate your macros ahead of time, so you don't need to calculate every time you consume your meals.

Preparation Before Meal Prep

What I love most about meal prep? It's fun and easy! Before you put on your chef hat and having fun in the kitchen, there are a few things that you need to do first.

- **Decide on what you want to eat:** Make a meal plan and indicate what you want to eat for the next few days. This is the most important step in meal prepping. Things that you need to do during the planning stage includes crating a list of ingredients to buy and kitchen equipment needed to make your food.

- **Shop for ingredients:** Go to the market or grocery store and buy the things that you need. Categorizing your list prevents you from missing that little ingredient needed to make one of the tasty dishes you plan on making. For instance, list all meats under one category so that you don't have to make a lot of trips in the market.

- **Organize the kitchen:** Before cooking, organize the kitchen by preparing the ingredients and the kitchen tools, utensils, and equipment that you need. This is also the time for kitchen preparations like chopping and marinating your ingredients.

- **Start cooking:** Once everything is ready, start cooking. Start with recipes that take a longer time to cook and do smaller things in between. That way, you will be able to use your time wisely.

The Art of Storing on Meal Prep

Storing is KING when it comes to meal prep. All your effort in cooking your tasty recipes would be for naught if you don't have proper storage containers your food. Remember, the dishes that you have prepared are perishable, thus you are at risk of being contaminated by pathogens like *E. coli* and *C. botulinum* that causes different food-borne diseases. So here are more tips to help you store your food properly—and keep them fresh tasting!

- **Store in separate containers:** Once the meals are cooked, store them separately in air-tight containers preferably those that are microwavable. Storing them in individual containers allow you to serve food by the time that you want to eat them. Moreover, storing them in separate containers means less exposure to contaminants.

- **Let meals cool to room temperature:** Allow your food to cool at room temperature before covering and storing them. The problem with putting a lid on the food while it is still hot is that it generates steam inside the container. This creates additional moisture inside the container such that it adds more variable for the bacteria to thrive inside the cooked meals.

- **Label the container:** Always label the container with the type of food, date, and other information that will serve as your guide on when and how to consume the food. It is also important to indicate the possible expiration date of the food. When labeling all containers, use a water-proof marker so that the markings will not be easily removed.

- **Store in the fridge:** The fridge should be kept at a temperature of 40°F and below. If you store it in the fridge, the food can last for 2 to 3 days. However, if you want food to last longer than a week, store it in the freezer. Your freezer should be set at 0°C and below.

- **Follow the first in, first out rule:** This means that consume the foods that were made first (or those that have the oldest manufactured date). Throw foods away that were not consumed after the "used by" date because the food might have gone bad. It may still look okay but don't take the risk.

- **Allow to thaw before heating:** When you are ready to consume your meals, take them out from the freezer and allow to thaw before heating in the microwave oven. But you have to take note that thawed food should be consumed within two days otherwise it might affect the final flavor of the food.

- **Always check your inventory:** You need to stay on high alert when it comes to spoiled food. Checking your meal prep inventory for any containers that may contain spoiled food can save your entire family from potentially ingesting bad food. Remember that just because you stored them in the fridge does not mean that you are already safe. Mold still grows even under refrigeration.

- **Always keep your refrigerator clean:** The refrigerator is a place where you keep raw meats and other ingredients. Cross contamination can happen if your refrigerator is dirty. So, if you want your prepared meals to be safe and fresh, make sure that you clean your fridge regularly with a mixture of soap and water and set aside a specific space to keep all your prepped meals so that you don't get mixed with the rest of the food items in your fridge.

Helpful Tips and Mistakes to Avoid

Worried that you might not be able to pull off cooking large amounts of food? Below are helpful tips and tricks as well as mistakes to avoid during meal prep.

- **Determine your goal:** Losing weight is the primary reason why you want to do meal prepping. But aside from that, what are your other goals? Do you want to follow a plant-based ketogenic diet or do clean eating? By knowing what your goals are, you can customize your meal prepping plans that will work for you.

- **Make simple recipes**: Opting for a one-pot dish can save you a lot of time and energy. Don't be too ambitious in the kitchen unless you are confident enough in your kitchen skills.

- **Use a spreadsheet**: Planning ahead becomes so much easier if you use the right tool – the spreadsheet. Don't be afraid to be called a nerd or an OCD just because you are so serious about your meal prepping plans. By using a spreadsheet, you will not only be able to make a meal plan but you can also use it to create a shopping list and calculate your macros.

- **Stock up your kitchen with the right tools**: Meal prepping is serious business and you need the right tools to get everything done. If you have a functional kitchen, then you already have the basics – pots, pans, instant pot, slow cooker, knives, ladles, and others. The tools that you need to stock up on are containers to store your food and enough space in the fridge to keep your food for longer.

- **Know your macros**: Knowing your macros is very important when making meal prep recipes. You can use nutrient calculators online such as the Macronutrient Calculator.

- **Mix and match your food**: Eating the same meals daily can eventually bore your palate. When doing meal prep recipes, make sure that you cook not only one ingredient but three or four. That way, you can mix and match your food so that you get different flavors every week. So for instance, if you made roasted chicken, make sure that you steam vegetables as well or make cauliflower rice.

- **Don't finish everything in one day**: Allocate a separate day for shopping and cooking so that you won't be overwhelmed with the process. By allocating certain days for shopping, prepping, and cooking meals, you will be able to enjoy making your meals instead of looking at it as a bothersome weekly task.

- **Not equipping your kitchen with the right tools**: When I mean "right tools," these include many storage containers, large (enough) pots and pans, and basic condiments like salt and pepper.

- **Not storing food properly**: The types of containers where you store your food can also affect the flavor and freshness of your food. Make sure that you opt for containers that are air-tight to retain the freshness of your food for longer. It is also important that you store your food in the fridge. If you are going to commute to work and you bring your meal prep recipes, store it in an insulated bag and place them inside the fridge (properly labeled as yours) if you are not eating it right away.

DIY Meal Prep for Your Daily Plan

Now that you know how easy it is to do meal prepping, making a meal prep daily plan should be easy enough. When you are making a daily plan, here are some principles that you need to practice:

- **Sourcing for ingredients:** Sourcing your ingredients is key to ketogenic meal prepping. The thing is that you cannot just use any other ingredients. As much as possible, try to use whole food ingredients so that you get most benefits out of your food. Whole food ingredients are raised without too much input such as additives, fertilizers, and pesticides so you can ensure your safety.

- **Use a meal template:** Using a template can help you plan your daily or weekly meals. To make a template, create a few columns and write down the recipes that you want for breakfast, lunch, and dinner. You can also add notes on your meal templates as well as schedule so that you can organize your shopping, prepping, and cooking.

- **Plan for short shopping trips:** Plan short shopping trips to complete your shopping list. Your life does not revolve around meal prep, so you don't need to dedicate your entire life on meal prepping. Work around your schedule. Shop during the weekend if you work full time or pass by the market on the way home to work to scout for ingredients.

Now that you know about the principles of making a DIY meal prep plan, it is time that you make your own.

Part 3. Understanding the Ketogenic Diet

I know! The ketogenic diet is the new buzzword in the world of dieting and fitness. But before you jump on the bandwagon and start implementing this diet, it is crucial that you have to understand what it is because it is only through understanding the diet will it really make wonders for you and your body.

What Is the Ketogenic Diet

I'll try to make this boring stuff not as tedious as it is, while still illuminating the basics and idea behind the keto diet.
Normally when we eat, our body processes the carbohydrates found in food to produce two compounds: (1) glucose and (2) insulin. Glucose is the simple sugar used by the cells as a source of energy while the insulin is the hormone produced by the pancreas that pushes the glucose in the bloodstream into the cells to be used up as energy.

Since glucose is the primary source of energy, any excess is not wasted by the body and is converted into fats and is stored in many organs particularly the adipose tissues, liver, and many others. This is the reason why consuming too many carbohydrates can cause obesity and other metabolic diseases like diabetes among many others. But what if there is a way to use up all these stored fats and convert it into energy? This is where the ketogenic diet comes in.

Ketosis is a natural physiological pathway and it is activated when our body does not consume any carbohydrates. In order to our survival, the body turns to fats and converts it to ketones so that it can still sustain itself despite the lack of food.

This is where the ketogenic diet comes in. Using the principles of ketosis, this particular diet regime mimics the ketogenic pathway without you ever getting hungry. Why? Because you can still eat food as long as they contain little to no carbohydrates.

The ketogenic diet encourages the body to produce ketones from fats in the liver that is then used by the body as a source of energy in the absence of glucose. The ketogenic diet uses up fat as the main source of energy.

Carbohydrates are not necessarily the culprit here but in order for ketosis to happen and encourage your body to burn stored fats, you have to stay away from it for the time being especially if you want to experience faster weight loss. By eating fewer carbs and more healthy fats (and adequate amount of protein), the body is induced to a state of ketosis thus making it easier to use up the fat reserves that the body already has on hand.

The ketogenic diet is more about changing your diet than fasting. So instead of consuming your usual meals, you need to change it such that you consume 60-75% fat, 15-30% protein, and 5% carbohydrates daily. By eating the right kinds of food, you trick your body into undergoing ketosis, yet you don't feel hungry at all.

Therefore, the goal of the ketogenic diet pushes your body into a state of ketosis by breaking down fats into ketones by eating the right amounts of food that support the fat-burning metabolic pathway.

Benefits of Ketogenic Diet

By now I know that you already have an inkling of the endless benefits of the keto diet. But, just to ensure that we are on the same page, here is a list of the wondrous benefits that you will gain with a keto diet.

- **Better mental focus:** Studies indicate that this particular diet can improve brain cognition and focus. While the brain uses glucose as its primary source of energy, it also loves to use up ketones. And since ketones do not spike blood sugar levels, the brain's condition is kept at its best performing level.

- **Better control of blood sugar levels:** When the body is at the state of ketosis, the pancreas takes a rest in pumping insulin. Once you give your pancreas a rest, the body becomes more sensitive to glucose. This particular diet regimen can help stabilize the blood sugar levels thus making it easier for people who suffer from Type 2 diabetes to manage your condition.

- **Reduce cravings:** Consumption of higher amounts of fat is more filling than carbohydrates thus the ketogenic diet can help reduce your cravings and hunger pains.

- **Better blood pressure and cholesterol levels:** Contrary to what most people think, consumption of healthy fats can lower down the levels of cholesterol and triglycerides in the body. Thus, the ketogenic diet has the ability to lower down the risk for cardiovascular diseases.

- **Clear the skin:** If you suffer from acne and other skin anomalies, the ketogenic diet can help improve the quality of your skin. In fact, there have been several studies that suggest that those who follow this regimen have better immune system thus your bodies can fight inflammation on all parts of the body including the skin.

- **Treatment for epilepsy:** Didn't you know that before it became famous as a weight loss diet, the ketogenic diet was first used to reduce the episodes of seizures among patients with epilepsy? Epileptic patients seem to respond well with the ketogenic diet and the ketones seem to have protective effects on the brain.

Is the Ketogenic Diet Suitable for Me?

On the other side of the spectrum, why not? While the ketogenic diet is one of the most popular diets out there, it is important to note that it is not a one-size-fits-all solution to all your health problems. Just like other types of diet programs, not everyone is encouraged to do it. And so, before you even start planning your meals, make sure that you ask yourself these questions in order to know if this is the diet for you.

- **How long can I follow the diet?** The ketogenic diet, unlike other fad diets, does not last for a week. In fact, you need to wait for months to be able to see results. So, if you cannot follow a diet program for a long time, then this diet is not definitely for you.

- **Will it fit my food preferences?** If you follow certain dietary guidelines such as veganism or vegetarianism, then this particular diet regimen might be hard to follow. Although not impossible, finding the right substitute without changing your macros can be hard especially if you are a newbie to this diet.

- **Do I suffer from medical conditions that will put me at risk?** Although the ketogenic diet is great for most people, those who suffer from kidney-related diseases should not go into this diet because the presence of fat and protein can have damaging effects on the kidneys.

So, is the ketogenic diet suitable for you? The answer depends on your condition and preference.

What to Eat on Keto Diet

The key to staying in ketosis is to eat the right kinds of food. It is important for dieters to strictly follow the ratio of 75% fat, 20% protein, and 5% carbs. Having said this, what kinds of foods are you allowed to eat while following this diet? Below is a list of foods that you should consume when following the ketogenic diet.

- **Healthy fats:** While fat is very important in the ketogenic diet, it is important to consume only good fats. These include coconut oil, MCT oil, olive oil, butter, avocado oil, ghee, and other dairy sources such as cream and cheese. The avocado fruit is also a source of healthy fat.

- **Meat and fish:** Meat and fish are rich in protein. Choose from red meats, salmon, pork, turkey, chicken, organ meat, tuna, and trout to name a few. However, make sure that you consume only a small amount of protein– preferably matchbox-sized.

- **Nuts and seeds:** Nuts and seeds are staple items for people who follow the ketogenic diet. Stock up your pantry with almond, cashew nuts, walnut, brazil nuts, pumpkin seeds, and chia seeds to name a few.

- **Eggs:** Eggs are good sources of protein and healthy fats.

- **Low carb vegetables:** Vegetables that have low carbohydrate content is allowed in this diet. You are good sources of fiber as well as vitamins and minerals. Low carb vegetables that are allowed for this diet include spinach, kale, beet greens, and other leafy greens. Other vegetables that you can eat include cucumber, tomatoes, onions, peppers, and cauliflowers.

- **Some fruits:** Some fruits are not allowed in the ketogenic diet because you contain high amounts of fructose. Although this may be the case, there are certain vegetables that you can include in this diet including limes, blueberries, lemons, apples, and strawberries. These fruits do not only have a low glycemic index but also contain high amounts of fiber, vitamins, minerals, and antioxidants.

- **Sweeteners:** Technically, most sweeteners are not allowed because you contain sugar but there are some sweeteners that are allowed for this particular diet regimen and these include stevia, erythritol, and monk fruit.

What Not to Eat

The ketogenic diet is very easy to follow contrary to popular belief. While there are many types of foods that you are not allowed to eat while following this diet, it is not really difficult to eliminate different food groups from your meals. Thus, below are the types of foods that you should avoid otherwise it will kick off ketosis.

- **Grain and starches:** Grains and starches are broken down into glucose thus you should be avoided. Avoid grains like oatmeal, rice, barley, rye, corn, wheat, and basically all types of grains that are available in the market.

- **Sugar:** Sugar – particularly free sugar–should be excluded from the ketogenic diet. Avoid honey, white sugar, maple syrup, molasses, and fruit sugar.

- **Fruits:** Most fruits contain high amounts of fructose–fruit sugar–thus, you should be avoided at all cost. This is especially true for fruits that contain high amounts of sugar such as watermelon and bananas.

- **Root vegetables:** Root vegetables such as potatoes, taro, sweet potatoes, parsnips, and carrots contain starch, which is converted to simple sugar.

- **Processed oil:** While the ketogenic diet encourages people to eat more fat, it discourages people to consume processed oils. These include canola oil, vegetable oil, soy oil, and corn oil.

- **Alcoholic beverages:** Alcoholic beverages contain high amounts of sugar thus making it bad for ketosis.

- **Beans and legumes:** While beans and legumes are an important source of vegetable protein, it is also high in starch that is converted into glucose. Avoid different types of beans such as kidney beans, red beans, peanuts, pinto beans, chickpeas, mung beans, and many others because you contain high amounts of starch.

Common Keto Ingredients for Meal Prep Shopping

Preparing keto-friendly meals can be very challenging especially for people who are new to this diet. But more than making meals, what makes this diet regimen challenging is shopping for the ingredients. Thus, to help you with meal prep, you need to know which kitchen staples you need to have. Below are common keto ingredients that you need to shop and stock up your pantry.

Oils and Condiments		Fruits
Avocado oil	celery salt	Avocado
Olive oil	red chili flakes	Lemon
Dijon mustard	ground cinnamon	Lime
Mayonnaise	ground nutmeg	Blueberries
Salt and pepper	ground all spice	Strawberries
Dried parsley powder	garlic	
Onion powder		
Vegetables		**Eggs and Dairy** (Cheese, Milk, Yogurt, Butter, etc.)
Broccoli		Eggs
Cauliflower		Half-and-half
Spinach		Heavy whipping cream
Kale		Sour cream
Watercress		Butter
Cucumber		Cheddar cheese
Onion		Parmesan cheese

Protein (Meat, Fish, Poultry, Beans, etc.)	Others
Bacon	Almond flour
Ground beef	Psyllium husk powder
Salmon	Powdered erythritol
Steak	Unsweetened coconut flakes
Chicken	Liquid stevia
Pork loin	Unsweetened cocoa powder

This is just an example of a grocery list that you can do to make keto meal prep recipes. You can buy them in most grocery stores but for specialty ingredients such as almond flour and psyllium powder, you can purchase them from specialty health stores or online. Good luck finding the ingredients that you need.

Part 4
Meal Prep

Meal Prep 1

The first two days on keto diet

Meal Prep 1: The first two days on keto diet

Fresh Food Shopping List for 2 Days	**Meat and seafood** 1 rotisserie chicken 1 (16-oz) package of bacon **Dairy:** 1 medium block of Parmigiano-Reggiano cheese 1 (8-oz.) pkg. of goat cheese 1 (8-oz.) container of mozzarella cheese 4 Cups of coconut milk 12 organic eggs **You May Already Have:** Coconut oil Salt Black pepper **Flour** 1 package of almond flour 1 Pacakge of coconut flour **Spices:** Ground cumin Ground cinnamon Cayenne pepper Chilli powder Powdered sugar	**Veggies** 1 Bunch of spinach 2 to 3 carrots 3 medium Zucchinis 1 lb of sweet potatoes 1 small yellow onion 1 small red onion 1 head of garlic 3 ripe avocado 2 limes 1 to 2 lemons Green olives Broccoli 8 oz. of baby Portobello mushrooms 1 head of broccoli 1 small bunch of fresh flat-leaf parsley 1 small bunch of fresh cilantro 1 small brunch of fresh thyme
Breakfast A	*Coconut Flour Northern Pancakes*	
Breakfast B	*Egg stuffed Portobello mushrooms*	
Lunch	*Ground Meat Casserole*	

Soup	***Broccoli Soup***
Snack	***Ground beef, cheese meatballs***
Dinner	***Tuscan Chicken***
Nutrition intake per day:	Calories: 1285	Fat: 250.3g	Carbohydrates: 20.7g	Protein 128.88 g	Sugar 9.9g

Breakfast: *Coconut Flour Northern Pancakes*

Preview:

Prep Time: 5 min
Cooking Time: 15 min
Total Time: 20 min
Serves: 1
Appliance: Skillet

Nutrition per Serving:

Calories: 380; Fat: 54.8 g
Carbs: 4 g; Protein 20.5 g
Sugar: 1.7 g;

Ingredients

- 1 cup of coconut flour
- 8 organic eggs
- 1 cup of Coconut Oil melted
- 1 and 1/2 cups of almond milk
- Almond butter for the topping
- Chopped strawberries

Cooking Direction:

1. Combine all the ingredients of the pancake
2. In about 2-3 tablespoons of size servings, cook your batter in a greased skillet with oil over a medium heat
3. Repeat the same process until all the batter is done
4. Evenly divide the pancakes between 2 storage containers with the diced strawberries
5. Top your pancakes with almond butter
6. Store your pancake in the refrigerator

Note: Please also note that absorbency of the coconut flour varied according to brands. So if your mixture is quite dry, you can add additional oil and remember to set the batter aside for 5 minutes before cooking it.

Storage, freeze, thaw and reheat guideline:

This .an be stored in the refrigerator at a temperature of about 37 °F in a glass or a plastic container for two meal prep days. When you want to consume this recipe, all you have to do is to reheat it in a skillet or in a microwave for about 5 minutes after it is thawed.

Breakfast: *Egg stuffed Portobello mushrooms*

Preview:

Prep Time: 10 min
Cooking Time: 5 min
Total Time: 15 min
Serves: 2
Appliance: Oven

Nutrition per Serving:

Calories: 165; Fat: 45.6 g
Carbs: 4.4 g; Protein 14.38 g
Sugar: 1.8 g;

Ingredients

- A Portobello
- An organic egg
- 2 cup of Mozzarella cheese
- Spinach
- 1 tablespoon of avocado oil

Cooking Direction:

1. Empty the Portobello and bake at 350 about 5 minutes.
2. Cook the egg during this time.
3. Add mozzarella in the hollow of the Portobello and brown until desired consistency.
4. Cut half a sliced avocado and sprinkle with chilli powder.
5. Remove the Portobello from the oven; place the egg on the grilled cheese.
6. Sit the Portobello on a bed of spinach and drizzle with olive oil and white vinegar dressing.
7. Season with salt and pepper to taste
8. Divide the Portobello mushrooms betweens 2 plastic containers

Storage, freeze, thaw and reheat guideline:

This .an be stored in the refrigerator at a temperature of about 39 °F in a glass or a plastic container for two meal prep days. And if you want to keep the taste of the mushroom fresh, you can place it in a towel; then place it in the containers. When you want to consume this recipe, all you have to do is to reheat it in a microwave for about 3 to 4 minutes.

9. Store the Portobello mushrooms in the refrigerator and top with chopped parsley each.	

Lunch: *Ground Meat Casserole*

Preview:

Prep Time: 7 min
Cooking Time: 5 min
Total Time: 12 min
Serves: 2
Appliance: oven

Nutrition per Serving:

Calories: 230; Fat: 76.9 g
Carbs: 6.2 g; Protein 25 g
Sugar: 2.1 g;

Ingredients

- ½ Pound of minced meat
- A small onion chopped with a knife
- 1 bowl of green, red and yellow peppers, diced
- 2 Cups of grated mozzarella
- 200 grams of Edam or grated Cheddar
- A pinch of hot pepper
- 1 diced tomato
- 3 tablespoons chopped coriander
- 2 tablespoons of olive oil
- 1 clove garlic minced

Cooking Direction:

1. Preheat the oven to 400° F.
2. Sauté the salt and pepper ground meat in a pan with a tablespoon of olive oil. Remove from heat and reserve the meat.
3. In the same pan, pour a tablespoon of olive oil, a clove of chopped garlic, onion and peppers, cook until the onion becomes translucent. There should be no liquid in the pan.
4. In a baking dish (a cast iron skillet, or a pan for paella), arrange a layer of meat, a vegetable and a cheese mixture.
5. Put a last layer of cheese and sprinkle with chilli.
6. Put in the oven for 10 minutes. The cheese must completely melt but it must not begin to harden.
7. Divide the dish between 2 containers and top each container with chopped contained and tomato slices
8. Store the containers in the refrigerator

Storage, freeze, thaw and reheat guideline:

This .an be stored in any refrigerator at 40 °F in a glass or disposable container for about two days. When you want to have this lunch, remove the container from the refrigerator and set aside for 5 minutes; then heat it for about 5 minutes in the oven.

Soup: *Broccoli Soup*

Preview:

Prep Time: 5 min
Cooking Time: 10 min
Total Time: 15 min
Serves: 2
Appliance: Stove

Nutrition per Serving:

Calories: 130; Fat: 23 g
Carbs: 2 g; Protein 8 g
Sugar: 1.3 g;

Ingredients

- 1 pound of broccoli, washed and cut
- ½ pound of zucchini, cut into cubes
- 1 leeks
- 2 tablespoons of coconut oil
- Salt pepper
- 1 cup of goat cheese

Cooking Direction:

1. In a casserole, put the coconut oil to melt
2. Add the chopped leek and melt.
3. Add the chopped vegetables while mixing well.
4. Wait until the vegetables are almost covered and cook for about 20 minutes. The vegetables must melt.
5. Divide the soup into 2 containers
6. Top with chopped parsley
7. Store the containers in the refrigerator

Storage, freeze, thaw and reheat guideline:

This .an be storage in refrigerator at 0 F in a glass or a plastic container for about two days. When you want to serve your soup, just remove it from the refrigerator and microwave it for about 5 minutes.

Snack: *Ground beef, cheese meatballs*

Preview:

Prep Time: 8 min
Cooking Time: 6 min
Total Time: 14 min
Serves: 2
Appliance: Frying pan

Nutrition per Serving:

Calories: 279; Fat: 28 g
Carbs: 2.3 g; Protein 44 g
Sugar: 2 g;

Ingredients

- 1 Pound of Ground Beef
- 1 Cup of goat Cheese
- 3 tablespoons Parmesan cheese
- 1 teaspoon Garlic Powder
- 1/2 teaspoon Salt
- 1/2 teaspoon Pepper

Cooking Direction:

- Cut the cheese into cubes
- Mix the dry ingredients with the ground beef
- Wrap the cubes of cheese in mince (1 pound of mince should make about 9 Balls)
- Pan Fry the meatballs.
- Cover with a lid to capture the heat all around.
- Divide the meatballs into 2 containers
- Seal the container and store it in the refrigerator

Storage, freeze, thaw and reheat guideline:

This meatball .an be storage in refrigerator at 38 °F in a plastic container for about 2 days. When you want to serve your snack, remove the balls from the refrigerator and microwave it for about 4 minutes.

Dinner: *Tuscan Chicken*

Preview:

Prep Time: 10 min
Cooking Time: 30 min
Total Time: 40 min
Serves: 2
Appliance: Stove

Nutrition per Serving:

Calories: 201; Fat: 22 g
Carbs: 1.8 g; Protein 26 g
Sugar: 1 g;

Ingredients

- 1 lb boneless and skinless chicken thighs
- 3 tablespoons of olive oil
- 6 green onions, chopped
- 1 1/2 cups white wine
-
- 1 1/2 cups chicken broth
- 1 branch of fresh rosemary
- 1/3 cup black and green olives, pitted and roughly chopped
- Salt and pepper

Cooking Direction:

1. In a large skillet, brown the chicken in the oil. Salt lightly (be careful, the olives are already salted) and pepper.
2. Add green onions and continue cooking for about 2 minutes. Add half of the white wine and simmer until evaporated.
3. Add half of the broth, rosemary and olives. Simmer on low heat until the liquid has reduced by half.
4. Add the remaining wine and broth gradually during cooking as soon as the liquid has reduced by half (see note). Return the chicken a few times during cooking to coat it well in the sauce.
5. Simmer over low heat for about 30 minutes, until the chicken becomes fluffy; check that with a fork and check if the sauce has thickened.
6. Adjust seasoning. Remove the rosemary branch.

Storage, freeze, thaw and reheat guideline:

This Tuscan Chicken .an be storage in refrigerator at 40 °F in a plastic container for about 2 days. When you want to consume your dinner, remove the chicken from the refrigerator and

7. Divide the chicken thighs between 2 containers 8. Lock the containers and store your dinner in the refrigerator	microwave it for about 5 minutes.

Meal Prep

2

The 3rd and 4th days on keto diet

Meal Prep 2: The 3rd and 4th days on keto diet

Fresh Food Shopping List for 2 Days	**Meat** 2.5 – 3 lb chicken breasts 12oz roll of breakfast sausage (sugar free) 1lb package ham 1lb ground turkey 1lb ground beef 1lb sugar free bacon **Vegetables:** 2 fresh tomatoes 1 red or yellow bell pepper 1 8oz package of baby spinach leaves 4 avocados 1 bunch of celery 2 heads of cauliflower 1 bunch fresh basil	**Dairy** Almond milk Coconut milk 16oz cheddar cheese 8 oz cream cheese 12 organic eggs 4 oz feta cheese 1/2 gallon unsweetened almond milk 16oz heavy cream 8oz package of string cheese 8oz package pepper jack cheese slices Coconut oil 4 oz parmesan cheese, grated
		Frozen 10 oz package frozen spinach 10 oz package frozen broccoli florets
Breakfast A	*Gluten free cereal*	
Breakfast B	*Mushroom Omelette with ham and cheese*	
Lunch	*Mussels with cream and bacon*	
Snack	*Stuffed Peppers*	
Dinner	*Chicken curry*	
Appetizer	*Crab, avocado and fennel skillet*	

| Nutrition intake per day: | Calories: 1626 \| Fat: 342.6g \| Carbohydrates: 30.5g \| Protein 159.8 g \| Sugar 12.5g |

Breakfast: *Gluten free cereal*

Preview:

Prep Time: 15 min

Cooking Time: 35 min
Total Time: 50 min
Serves: 2
Appliance: Oven

Nutrition per Serving:

Calories: 201; Fat: 24 g
Carbs: 1.8 g; Protein 26 g
Sugar: 1 g;

Ingredients

- 1 cup almond milk
- 1 cup of almond powder
- 2 tbsp. tablespoon of coconut oil or melted butter
- 2 tbsp. tablespoon of coconut flour
- 1 to 2 organic egg whites
- 1 to 2 tbsp. cinnamon powder (according to your taste)
- 1 pinch of salt
- Optional: stevia or honey to sweeten

Cooking Direction:

1. Preheat the oven to 300 °F.
2. Place all ingredients in a large bowl with the exception of the second egg white.
3. Mix with a spatula to obtain a homogeneous paste, not too sticky or too hard. If necessary, add the second egg white to change the texture.
4. Place the dough between two sheets of baking paper and spread it finely with the rolling pin.
5. Bake for 5 minutes so that the dough begins to harden, remove the dish from the oven and cut small squares.
6. Bake again for 10 minutes then turn off the oven and allow the cereals to continue drying and harden inside, about 35 minutes.
7. Divide the squares between 2 plastic containers
8. Store the containers in the refrigerator

Storage, freeze, thaw and reheat guideline:

This gluten free cereal .an be stored in a refrigerator at a temperature of 40 °F in a container for 2 days. When you want to have your breakfast; just remove the containers from the refrigerator and set it aside for 5 minutes.

Breakfast: *Mushroom Omelette with ham and cheese*

Preview:

Prep Time: 10 min
Cooking Time: 5 min
Total Time: 15 min
Serves: 2
Appliance: Stove

Nutrition per Serving:

Calories: 322; Fat: 46.7 g
Carbs: 4 g; Protein 17 g
Sugar: 0.2 g;

Ingredients

- 1 organic egg
- 1 tablespoon of cheese cream
- 1 cup of ham
- 2 cups of mushrooms
- 2 Tablespoons of coconut oil
- ½ cup of goat cheese

Cooking Direction:

1. Mix in a bowl the egg and the cream
2. Melt the oil in a small pan
3. Add the mushrooms and cook for about 3 minutes
4. Add the ham, mix well
5. Pour the egg mixture into the pan and cook for 2 minutes
6. Add small portions of your goat cheese and add it to the pan
7. Lower the heat and cover for 1 minute to allow the goat to melt

Storage, freeze, thaw and reheat guideline:

This breakfast .an be stored in a refrigerator at a temperature of 38 °F in a container for about 2 days. When you want to enjoy your breakfast; all you have to do is to remove the containers from the refrigerator and reheat it for about 3 to 4 minutes.

Lunch: *Mussels with cream and bacon*

Preview:

Prep Time: 10 min
Cooking Time: 10 min
Total Time: 20 min
Serves: 2
Appliance: Stove

Nutrition per Serving:

Calories: 350; Fat: 92.8 g
Carbs: 8.7 g; Protein 48 g
Sugar: 3 g;

Ingredients

- 1 Pound of mussels
- 1 cup of smoked blue cheese
- 2 tablespoons of chopped shallots
- 250 ml of cream cheese
- 4 Oz of white mushrooms
- 2 slices of bacon
- 2 Tablespoons of coconut oil
- 250 ml of low carbohydrate white wine

Cooking Direction:

1. In a large saucepan, sauté the shallots in the butter for about 2 minutes
2. Add the wine and bring to a boil.
3. Add the mussels, cover and cook for about 5 minutes until the mussels are open.
4. Remove the mussels and place them in your serving dish
5. Discard the mussels that have remained closed

TO MAKE THE SAUCE CREAM OF BLUE SMOKE AND BACON

6. Sauté the bacon, the shallot and the mushrooms until bacon is crisp.
7. Add the cream and the blue cheese.
8. Stir and cook for 3-4 minutes.
9. Divide the mussels between 2 containers
10. Add the cream to the 2 containers
11. Store your lunch in the refrigerator.

Storage, freeze, thaw and reheat guideline:

This lunch .an be stored in your refrigerator at a temperature of 40 °F in 2 containers for 2 days. When you want to serve your lunch; just remove the containers from the refrigerator and reheat the mussels lunch for 5 minutes.

Snack: *Stuffed Peppers*

Preview:	Nutrition per Serving:
Prep Time: 15 min Cooking Time: 60 min Total Time: 75 min Serves: 2 Appliance: Stove	Calories: 268; Fat: 70.3 g Carbs: 6.5 g, Protein 23g Sugar: 2.7 g

Ingredients

- 4 peppers
- ½ pound of sausage meat
- ½ ground beef
- 2 onions
- 2 cloves garlic
- 1 branch of parsley
- 1 organic egg
- Thyme
- Pepper
- Salt
- 3 slices of gluten free bread
- ½ cup of coconut milk

Cooking Direction:

1. Finely chop the onions, garlic and parsley.
2. Dip the gluten free bread in warm milk to soften it and mix all the ingredients.
3. Wash the peppers and hollow out the tail.
4. Put in a dish in the oven at 390 °F for 60 minutes; turn the peppers halfway through cooking.
5. Add 1 pinch of salt
6. Divide the stuffed peppers between 2 containers
7. Store the containers in the refrigerator

Storage, freeze, thaw and reheat guideline:

To store stuffed peppers in the refrigerator, place it in the containers and then place it in your refrigerator at a temperature of about 38 °F in 2 containers for about 2 days. When you want to serve this snack; remove the containers from the refrigerator and reheat the stuffed peppers in the microwave for about 3 minutes.

Dinner: *Chicken curry*

Preview:

Prep Time: 10 min
Cooking Time: 30 min
Total Time: 40 min
Serves: 2
Appliance: Stove

Nutrition per Serving:

Calories: 323; Fat: 53.2 g
Carbs: 5 g; Protein 27.8 g
Sugar: 3 g;

Ingredients

- 2 chicken breasts
- 1 garlic clove
- 1 small onion
- 1 zucchini
- 2 carrots
- 1 box of bamboo shoots or sprouts
- 1 cup of coconut milk
- 1 Tablespoon of tomato paste
- 2 tablespoons of yellow curry paste

Cooking Direction:

1. Mince the onion and sauté in a pan with a little oil for a few minutes.
2. Add chicken cut in large cubes and crushed garlic, salt, pepper and sauté quickly over high heat until meat begins to color.
3. Pour zucchini and carrots in thick slices into the pan.
4. Sear over high heat for a few minutes, then add the coconut milk, tomato sauce, bamboo shoots and one to two tablespoons of curry paste, depending on your taste.
5. Cook over low heat and cover for 30 to 45 minutes, stirring occasionally
6. Once cooked, divide the chicken curry between 2 containers
7. Store the containers in the refrigerator

Storage, freeze, thaw and reheat guideline:

To store the chicken curry in the refrigerator, transfer it to containers and cover it with a layer of oil; then make sure the temperature of refrigerator is 39 °F. When you want to serve this dinner, just remove it from the refrigerator and reheat it in a pan for about 5 minutes.

Appetizer: *Crab, avocado and fennel skillet*

Preview:

Prep Time: 5 min
Cooking Time: 10 min
Total Time: 15 min
Serves: 2
Appliance: Stove

Nutrition per Serving:

Calories: 162; Fat: 55.6g
Carbs: 4.5 g; Protein 18 g
Sugar: 2.6 g;

Ingredients

- 2 big avocados
- 2 tbsp of fennel, cut into small cubes
- 1 tbsp chopped chives
- 2 tablespoons freshly squeezed lemon juice
- 1 tsp mayonnaise
- 6 drops of hot sriracha sauce
- 2 tablespoon olive oil
- ½ tomato cut into small cubes
- Salt and pepper to taste
- Flesh of a crab.

Cooking Direction:

1. Mix all ingredients together except the crab meat
2. Using a cookie cutter, assemble the avocado tartar
3. Add the crabmeat
4. To assemble your dish, divide the avocado tarts into 2 plastic containers
5. Store the containers in the refrigerator

Storage, freeze, thaw and reheat guideline:

To store this appetizer in the refrigerator, carefully place it in containers; then place the containers in the refrigerator and set the temperature to about 38 °F. When you want to serve your appetizer, remove it from the refrigerator and microwave it for about 2 to 3 minutes.

Meal Prep 3

The 5th, 6th, and 7th days on keto diet

Meal Prep 3: The 5th, 6th, and 7th days on keto diet		
Fresh Food Shopping List for 3 Days	**Vegetables:** 4 white leeks 3 Onions 1 Pound of bacon 24 Organic eggs 6 avocados 2 mangos 1 pound of fresh tomatoes 2 limes 3 heads of garlic 1 Bunch of fresh mint Dill Fresh basil Radish 6 zucchinis Chopped chives Chopped oregano	**Meat and fish** 8 anchovy fillets 2 salmon fillets 4 slices smoked salmon 1 Pound of chicken wings **Dairy products** 12 organic eggs Coconut milk 2 almond flour bagels 2 cups parmesan cheese 1 cup cheddar cheese Fresh goat cheese
	Oil: Coconut oil Avocado oil	**Other spices:** Mayonnaise Lemon juice Dijon Mustard White wine vinegar Celery seed Cayenne pepper Maple syrup
Breakfast	Low carb Ketogenic Frittata	
Salad	Cesar salad with bacon and vinaigraitte	
Lunch	Grilled salmon with avocado	
Lunch	Buffalo chicken wings	
Snack	Stuffed zucchini	
Dinner	Almond flour Burger with goat cheese	

| Nutrition intake per day: | Calories: 1359 | Fat: 259.7g | Carbohydrates: 13.5g | Protein 95.1 g | Sugar 6.48g |

Breakfast: *Low carb Ketogenic Frittata*

Preview:

Prep Time: 5 min
Cooking Time: 5 min
Total Time: 10 min
Serves: 3
Appliance: Oven

Nutrition per Serving:

Calories: 205; Fat: 28g
Carbs: 2 g; Protein 14 g
Sugar: 1 g

Ingredients

- 3 white leeks
- 1 big onion
- 1 Pound of diced bacon
- 8 Organic eggs

Cooking Direction:

1. Finely mince the onion.
2. Wash the leeks thoroughly and cut into thin slices.
3. Cook the vegetables over low heat, about 15 minutes, in a pan with lid (with just a little olive oil).
4. Stir regularly.
5. When the leeks / onions mixture is cooked, add the bacon and stir on high heat, stirring briskly.
6. In a few minutes, the bacon will cook while impregnating the vegetables
7. Stop cooking and reserve.
8. In a bowl, beat 8 organic eggs and season with salt and pepper.
9. Add the vegetables and mix everything.
10. Pour into a buttered baking tin and bake for about 5 minutes at 400 °F.
11. Wait 5 minutes before unmolding.
12. Cut into large squares and serve with a salad for an evening meal.
13. Divide the squares between 3 containers
14. Store the containers in the refrigerator

Storage, freeze, thaw and reheat guideline:

To store this breakfast, put it in containers; then put the containers in the refrigerator at a freezing temperature of 38 °F. When you are ready to serve your breakfast, remove it from the refrigerator and microwave the frittata for about 5 minutes.

Salad: *Cesar salad with bacon and vinaigraitte*

Preview:

Prep Time: 10 min
Cooking Time: 0 min
Total Time: 10 min
Serves: 3
Appliance: Not cooked

Nutrition per Serving:

Calories: 180; Fat: 55.3 g
Carbs: 5.2 g, Protein 5.5 g
Sugar: 1.38 g

Ingredients

To make the vinaigrette
- 2 and ½ cup of coconut oil (or replace with olive oil)
- 1/4 cup avocado oil or olive oil
- 9 anchovy fillets
- 2 and ½ tablespoons of mayonnaise
- 2 tablespoons of lemon juice
- 1 tablespoon Dijon mustard
- 1 tablespoon white wine vinegar
- 2 garlic cloves
- 1 pinch of salt
- 1 Pinch of pepper
- Bacon or pork rinds

Cooking Direction:

1. Place all ingredients in a blender.
2. Pulse for 1 minute
3. Reserve the vinaigrette aside.
4. Ingredients for the salad:
5. 4 cups of Roman salad
6. 6 slices of crispy bacon
7. 8 pieces of pork rind
8. 1 cup goat cheese
9. In a bowl, mix the salad and the desired amount of Caesar dressing.
10. Place in the salad bowls.
11. Add bacon, parmesan and pieces of pork rind.
12. To assemble your salad; divide it between 3 containers
13. Top each container with the vinaigrette and store in the refrigerator!

Storage, freeze, thaw and reheat guideline:

To store this salad, put it in containers; then place the containers in the refrigerator at a temperature of 37 °F. When you are ready to serve your breakfast, remove it from the refrigerator and set it aside for 4 minutes.

Lunch: *Grilled salmon with avocado*

Preview:

Prep Time: 5 min
Cooking Time: 10 min
Total Time: 15 min
Serves: 3
Appliance: oven

Nutrition per Serving:

Calories: 315; Fat: 71.4 g
Carbs: 6.3 g, Protein 34.6 g
Sugar: 0.8 g

Ingredients

- 2 salmon fillets
- 2 avocados
- 1 mango
- 2 tomatoes
- 1 lime
- 1/2 bunch of fresh mint
- 1 pinch of chilli powder
- 4 c. tablespoon of olive oil
- Salt pepper

Cooking Direction:

1. Peel and stone the avocado then cut the flesh into cubes. Peel the mango, remove the flesh and cut it into cubes. Wash the tomatoes and cut them too. Wash and chop the mint.
2. Mix all these ingredients in a bowl. Add the squeezed lemon juice and 2 tbsp. tablespoon of olive oil, chilli, salt and pepper. Mix gently and reserve in a cool place.
3. Heat the rest of the oil in a non-stick pan and cook the salmon patties about 3 minutes on each side, or more depending on the desired cooking.
4. Season with salt and pepper
5. To assemble your lunch, divide the salmon between the 3 containers
6. Top each container with the mango and avocado salsa
7. Place the containers in the refrigerator and store until consumption

Storage, freeze, thaw and reheat guideline:

To store this lunch, put it in containers; then place the containers in the refrigerator at a temperature of 40 °F. When you are ready to serve your lunch, remove it from the refrigerator and reheat it in a skillet for about 3 minutes.

Lunch : *Buffalo chicken wings*

Preview:

Prep Time: 5 min
Cooking Time: 15 min
Total Time: 20 min
Serves: 3
Appliance: oven

Nutrition per Serving:

Calories: 130; Fat: 26 g
Carbs: 2 g, Protein 16 g
Sugar: 1.4 g

Ingredients

- 6 chicken wings (cut off the end)
- 1/2 teaspoon avocado oil
- 1/8 teaspoon celery seed
- 1/4 teaspoon Cayenne pepper
- 1/8 teaspoon garlic salt
- 6 tablespoons pepper sauce
- 1 teaspoon white vinegar
- 1/2 teaspoon maple syrup
- 1 teaspoon or 2 Tabasco

Cooking Direction:

1. Heat the oil and cook the wings in small amounts.
2. Place the chicken wings on paper towels when they are cooked.
3. In a small saucepan, put all the ingredients in the sauce and heat gently. Mix well.
4. When all wings are cooked, place in a freezer bag and drizzle with sauce.
5. Coat sauce wings well while stirring.
6. Put on a grid on a cookie sheet and place the wings on it.
7. Bake at 425 ° F for about 15 minutes.
8. Once the chicken is ready, divide it between 3 containers or plastic bags and store it in the refrigerator for 2days

Storage, freeze, thaw and reheat guideline:

To store this lunch, place the chicken wings in containers or in small plastic bags; then place the containers in your refrigcrator and set the temperature to a temperature of 38 °F. When you are ready to serve your lunch, remove it from the refrigerator and set it reheat it in the oven for about 4 minutes.

Snack: *Stuffed zucchini*

Preview:

Prep Time: 10 min
Cooking Time: 20 min
Total Time: 30 min
Serves: 3
Appliance: oven

Nutrition per Serving:

Calories: 249; Fat: 25 g
Carbs: 1.8 g, Protein 13 g
Sugar: 1 g

Ingredients

- 5 small zucchini, washed and cut in half lengthwise
- 3 cloves of garlic, minced
- 2 fresh tomatoes, diced
- 1 and ½ tablespoon olive oil
- 1 tbsp fresh basil, chopped
- 1 tablespoon chopped fresh chives
- 1 tablespoon fresh oregano, chopped
- 1/4 cup grated parmesan cheese
- 1 cup cheddar cheese, grated
- 1 cup almond flour
- 1 organic egg

Cooking Direction:

1. Preheat oven to 375 ° F. Cut the zucchini in half and take the flesh with a spoon, being careful not to remove too much.
2. Chop the zucchini flesh and place in a large bowl. Add garlic, tomatoes, olive oil, basil, chives, oregano (reserve a small amount of herbs for finishing), half the amount of parmesan cheese and cheddar cheese. Mix well. Add the almond flour, salt and pepper. Add the egg and mix again.
3. Stuff zucchini and sprinkle with remaining herbs and cheese.
4. Bake for 15 to 20 minutes or until zucchini is cooked and filling is golden brown
5. When the zucchini is cooked, divide it into glass or plastic containers
6. Store the stuffed zucchini in the refrigerator

Storage, freeze, thaw and reheat guideline:

To store the stuffed zucchini, carefully arrange it in 3 containers lined with paper towels and place the containers in the refrigerator at 39° F. When you want to reheat your snack, it is very easy, just remove the containers from the refrigerator and microwave the zucchini for about 5 minutes.

Dinner: *Almond flour Burger with goat cheese*

Preview:

Prep Time: 10 min
Cooking Time: 20 min
Total Time: 30 min
Serves: 2
Appliance: Toaster

Nutrition per Serving:

Calories: 280; Fat: 54 g
Carbs: 4 g, Protein 12 g
Sugar: 0.9 g

Ingredients

- 2 almond flour bagels
- 2 tbsp of fresh goat cheese
- 4 slices smoked salmon
- 2 pinch Salt and pepper
- 4 Radishes
- Dill

Cooking Direction:

1. Cut the gluten free bagel in half. Put the two halves in the toaster to make them crisp.
2. Spread both slices of fresh goat cheese and add salmon.
3. Garnish the bagel with the radish and dill.
4. A pinch of salt and pepper and it's ready
5. Put each burger in a container and store in the refrigerator

Storage, freeze, thaw and reheat guideline:

To store the burgers and bagels, put it in a plastic wrap or bag and place it in the freezer. When you want to reheat your dinner, remove the plastic bag from the freezer and set it aside for 4 minutes. Heat the burger in the refrigerator for 5 minutes

Meal Prep

4

8th and 9th day of the Keto diet

Meal Prep 4: The 8th and 9th day of the Keto diet

Fresh Food Shopping List for 2 Days	**Meat and fish** Sugar-free bacon Ground beef 1 roast chicken Sugar-free sausage 5-3lb. roasted boneless beef chuck	**Frozen products:** 10 oz. packet of frozen broccoli florets 10 oz. packet of frozen spinach **Spices** 2 Heads of garlic Salt
	Dairy products: 3 dozen eggs ½ lb almond butter Thick cream ½ gallon of unsweetened almond milk 4 oz. grated parmesan cheese 8 oz packet pepper jack cheese slices 8 oz of sting cheese 8 oz of cream cheese Cheddar cheese 8 oz of sour cream	**Produce:** Bunch of fresh basil 6 avocados An 8 oz packet of spinach leaves 2 cauliflowers 1 bunch of celery 2 packages of romaine lettuce hearts 1 red or yellow pepper 2 tomatoes Xanthan gum
Breakfast A	Ketogenic biscuits with cheese sauce	
Breakfast B	Raspberry breakfast bowls	
Lunch	Asian style beef zoodles	
Soup	Leek and salmon soup	
Snack	Broccoli cheese balls	

Dinner	Sausage skillet with cabbage
Nutrition intake per day:	Calories: 1560	Fat: 586.2g	Carbohydrates: 50.9g	Protein 149.4 g	Sugar 6.5g

Breakfast: Ketogenic biscuits with cheese sauce

Preview:

Prep Time: 10 min
Cooking Time: 15 min
Total Time: 25 min
Serves: 1
Appliance: Oven

Nutrition per Serving:

Calories: 270; Fat: 106 g
Carbs: 9 g, Protein 32g
Sugar: 1.8 g

Ingredients

- 1 cup of melted coconut oil
- 4 large organic eggs
- 1/3 cup of coconut flour
- 1/4 teaspoon of salt
- 1/4 teaspoon of baking powder
- 1 cup grated goat cheese
- Low carb sausage sauce
- 1 pound of ground sausage
- 1 cup chicken broth
- 2 cup thick cream
- 1/2 teaspoon of xanthan gum
- Salt and pepper to taste

Cooking Direction:

1. Preheat your oven to 400°F. Line a baking dish with parchment, silicone baking mat or cooking spray.
2. Add all the ingredients of the biscuit in a large bowl and mix. Scoop the dough using a tablespoon of 3 tablespoons or tablespoon of 3 tablespoons of dough for each cookie. Place them 2 inches apart on the baking sheet. You can shape 9 cookies or more.
3. Bake for 15 minutes or until golden brown. Remove and set aside.
4. While the cookies are cooking, make the sauce.
5. In large skillet, brown and crumble sausage over medium-high heat until cooked through.
6. Add chicken broth, cream and xanthan gum. Mix to combine. Bring to a boil, reduce heat to low and continue to simmer until sauce is thick. Season with salt and pepper. Remove from fire.
7. To assemble your dish, cut your biscuits into halves; then divide the biscuits between 2 containers and pour the sauce on each container
8. Make sure to lock the containers; then store it in the refrigerator.

Storage, freeze, thaw and reheat guideline:

To store your biscuits, put it in a glass or a plastic container and place the container in the refrigerator at a temperature of 38 °F. And when you want to reheat the biscuits, remove it from the refrigerator and reheat it in the oven for about 5 minutes.

Breakfast: *Raspberry breakfast bowls*

Preview:

Prep Time: 10 min
Cooking Time: 0 min
Total Time: 10 min
Serves: 1
Appliance: microwave

Nutrition per Serving:

Calories: 298; Fat: 167 g
Carbs: 12 g, Protein 28.6 g
Sugar: 2 g

Ingredients

- 10 oz of mango or frozen peaches
- 1 cup of water
- 10 oz of frozen raspberries
- 1 cup light coconut milk
- 1/3 cup chia seeds
- 1/4 cup of flax flour
- 1/4 cup of honey
- 1 pinch of salt

Cooking Direction:

1. Soften the frozen fruits in the microwave or leave them on the counter for a little while.
2. Mix peaches with water. Mix the raspberries with the coconut milk.
3. Mix the two blends of fruit puree and incorporate the chia seeds, flax, honey and salt.
4. Let stand 10-15 minutes to thicken.
5. Time to assemble your meal prep breakfast and to do that, divide the blend between two containers and top it with your favourite fruits like strawberries and other toppings of your choice
6. Seal the containers and store it in the refrigerator for up to two days

Storage, freeze, thaw and reheat guideline:

To store the raspberry bowls, put it in 2 containers and place the containers in the refrigerator at a temperature of 39 °F. And when you want to reheat it add water to the containers to rehydrate them (the chia seeds absorb a lot of moisture, which makes them very thick).

Lunch: *Asian style beef zoodles*

Preview:

Prep Time: 10 min
Cooking Time: 7 min
Total Time: 17 min
Serves: 2
Appliance: stove

Nutrition per Serving:

Calories: 252; Fat: 122 g
Carbs: 14 g, Protein 36 g
Sugar: 1 g

Ingredients

- 4 large zucchini or 5 medium zucchinis
- 3 tablespoons of avocado oil or coconut oil
- 3 tablespoons chopped fresh ginger
- 5 minced cloves of garlic
- ½ cup chopped shallots
- 1-2 red peppers * diced
- 16 oz of beef sirloin
- ½ cup of coconut aminos
- 2 tablespoons of honey
- 1 tablespoon white wine vinegar
- 1 tablespoon fish sauce
- Juice of 1/2 lime about 1 tbsp.
- 1 cup of chopped carrots
- 1 cup of fresh basil

Cooking Direction:

1. Spiralize the zucchini noodles and set aside in a large plate or bowl.
2. Heat a large wok or skillet over medium-high heat. Add the oil and add the ginger, garlic and shallots. Cook 2-3 minutes or until fragrant, add the beef and chopped red pepper. Cook the beef for a few minutes, making sure each side is browned but not overcooked. Lower the fire to low.
3. Make the sauce by mixing all together the coconut aminos, the honey, the vinegar and fish sauce in a medium bowl.
4. Mix in the pa, with the beef. Stir in the noodles and mix to coat.
5. Finally, mix the carrots and fresh basil
6. To assemble your dish, divide the zoodles between containers and store it in the refrigerator

Storage, freeze, thaw and reheat guideline:

To store the zoodles in the refrigerator, place the containers in the refrigerator and store at a temperature of 38 °F. When you want to serve your lunch, remove it from the refrigerator and reheat it in a skillet for 3 minutes.

Soup: *Leek and salmon soup*	
Preview: Prep Time: 5 min Cooking Time: 10 min Total Time: 15 min Serves: 2 Appliance: stove	**Nutrition per Serving:** Calories: 240; Fat: 71 g Carbs: 6 g, Protein 24 g Sugar: 1.2 g

Ingredients

- 2 tablespoons of avocado oil
- 4 leeks, washed, trimmed and cut into croissants
- 3 cloves garlic minced
- 6 cups of seafood OR chicken broth
-
- 2 tbsp. Dried thyme leaves
- 1 lb. salmon, in bite size chunks (Thawed frozen salmon works great here)
- 1 cup of coconut milk
- Salt and pepper to taste

Cooking Direction: 1. Heat the avocado oil in a large saucepan or Dutch oven over low-medium heat. 2. Add the chopped leeks and garlic and cook until lightly softened. 3. Pour into the broth and add the thyme. Simmer for about 15 minutes and season with salt and pepper. 4. Add the salmon and coconut milk to the pan. 5. Return to low heat and cook until the fish is opaque and tender. 6. Set the soup aside to cool for 5 minutes 7. Divide the soup between 2 containers 8. Seal the containers very well; then store it in the refrigerator for 2 days	**Storage, freeze, thaw and reheat guideline:** To store this soup, put the containers in your refrigerator and store the temperature of about 39 °F. When you want to serve the soup; remove it from the refrigerator and reheat it in a pan over a medium heat for 4 minutes

Snack: *Broccoli cheese balls*

Preview:

Prep Time: 10 min
Cooking Time: 15 min
Total Time: 25 min
Serves: 2
Appliance: stove

Nutrition per Serving:

Calories: 175; Fat: 63 g
Carbs: 5 g, Protein 13g
Sugar: 1 g

Ingredients

- ¾ cup of almond flour
- ¼ cup + 3 tablespoons flax seed meal
- 4 ounces fresh broccoli
- 4 oz of mozzarella cheese
- 2 big eggs
- 2 teaspoons of yeast
- Salt and pepper to taste
- The sauce
- ¼ cup mayonnaise
- ¼ cup fresh chopped dill
- ½ tablespoon lemon juice
- Salt and pepper to taste

Cooking Direction:

1. Add broccoli to a food processor and mix until broccoli is completely destroyed.
2. Combine cheese, almond flour, ¼ cup flaxseed and baking powder with broccoli. If you want to add extra seasonings (salt and pepper), do it at this point.
3. Add the eggs and mix well until everything is incorporated.
4. Roll the mixture into balls, then coat with 3 tablespoons flaxseed meal.
5. Heat your fryer to 375°F; then place the balls inside the basket, without covering it too much.
6. Fry the balls until golden, about 3-5 minutes.
7. Make a zesty dill and lemon mayonnaise for a dip.
8. To assemble your dish, divide the broccoli balls between 2 containers and top each with the mayonnaise dip
9. Store the containers in the refrigerator!

Storage, freeze, thaw and reheat guideline:

To store your broccoli balls, place it in resealable plastic bags; then place the bags in containers and store it in the refrigerator at 38 °F. When you want to reheat your snack, it is very easy, all you have to do is to remove it from the refrigerator and microwave it for 4 minutes.

Dinner: *Sausage skillet with cabbage*

Preview:

Prep Time: 5 min
Cooking Time: 13 min
Total Time: 18 min
Serves: 2
Appliance: stove

Nutrition per Serving:

Calories: 325; Fat: 57.2 g
Carbs: 4.9 g, Protein 15.8 g
Sugar: 1.3 g

Ingredients

- 1 tablespoon of olive oil
- 3/4 cup shredded green cabbage
- 3/4 cup grated red cabbage
- 1/4 cup diced onion
- 2 spicy sausages (120g)
- 1/4 cup grated mozzarella
- 1 tablespoon fresh and chopped parsley
- Salt and pepper to taste
- Sausage and sausage with cabbage

Cooking Direction:

1. Place a large skillet on a stove over medium-high heat and heat olive oil. Immerse the cabbage and onion in the heated oil. Let stand for about 8-10 minutes or until vegetables are tender.
2. Chop the sausage into bite-size pieces. Mix with cabbage and onion and let stand another 8 minutes.
3. Spread the cheese over the top
4. Cover the skillet with a lid and set aside for 5 minutes to melt.
5. Remove the lid and mix your ingredients. Garnish with salt, pepper and parsley before serving.
6. To assemble the dish, divide the mixture between 2 containers; then store it in the refrigerator

Storage, freeze, thaw and reheat guideline:

To store your dinner and to maximize the life of your cabbage dish, for better safety and better quality, refrigerate your dish in airtight containers with aluminium foil at a temperature of 40°F.

Meal Prep

5

The 10th and 11th days on keto diet

Meal Prep 5: The 10th and 11th days on keto diet		
Fresh Food Shopping List for 2 Days	**Meat and fish** 4 oz and 11 slices of Bacon 1 pound Beef, chuck roast 25 oz of Beef, ground 23 organic eggs 1 pound shrimp 4 Ounces of roast beef 12 ounces of Sausage 12 oz of White fish, fillet **Dairy Products** 6 cups of Almond milk, unsweetened Goat cheese - 2 ounces Almond Butter -2 cups Cheddar cheese, shredded -2 cups Cream cheese – 3 cups Mozzarella, shredded - 2 cups	**Vegetables** 2 heads Broccoli 1 head Cabbage 1 head of Cauliflower 5 Celery stalks Fennel Garlic Spinach 1 pound of Zucchinis **Berries and fruits** 6 Avocados 2 cups of blackberry 1/2 cups of blueberry 1 cup cranberry 2 cups raspberry 3 cups of strawberry Tomato
	Oils 3 cups almond Butter 1 cup avocado Oil ½ cup coconut Oil ½ cup full fat Mayonnaise Olive Oil Vinegar	
Breakfast A	Low carb, Ketogenic waffles	
Breakfast B	Chia Pudding	
Lunch	Shrimp and broccoli paella	
Soup	Vegetable soup	
Snack	Deviled eggs	
Dinner	Chicken and broccoli gratin	

| Nutrition intake per day: | Calories: 1338 | Fat: 612.3g | Carbohydrates: 50.8g | Protein 106.3 g | Sugar 9.4g |

Breakfast: *Low carb, Ketogenic waffles*

Preview:

Prep Time: 5 min
Cooking Time: 5 min
Total Time: 10 min
Serves: 2
Appliance: stove

Nutrition per Serving:

Calories: 318; Fat: 73 g
Carbs: 6 g, Protein 10.9 g
Sugar: 1.9 g

Ingredients

- 1 cup of almond powder
- 1 cup of coconut milk
- 3 organic eggs
- 2 tablespoons of melted coconut milk
- A few drops of liquid vanilla extract
- 1 tsp of bicarbonate or baking powder

Cooking Direction:

1. Preheat your waffle maker
2. Mix all the ingredients in a bowl with a whisk, an electric mixer, or put all this in a blender of your choice.
3. Ketogenic waffles
4. Pour a ladle of dough per waffle iron and cook for a few minutes until the waffles are puffed and golden.
5. Cool on a rack; then assemble your breakfast by dividing the waffles between two containers
6. Top the waffles with strawberries and blueberries
7. Store the waffles in the refrigerator!

Storage, freeze, thaw and reheat guideline:

To store the waffles in the refrigerator, place it in containers and put the containers in the refrigerator at a temperature of about 39°F.

Breakfast: *Chia Pudding*

Preview:

Prep Time: 5 min
Cooking Time: 10 min
Total Time: 15 min
Serves: 2
Appliance: stove

Nutrition per Serving:

Calories: 105; Fat: 88 g
Carbs: 7.8 g, Protein 5.2 g
Sugar: 0 g

Ingredients

- 4 tablespoons of Chia seeds
- 240 ml unsweetened almond milk
- 1 teaspoon vanilla powder
- 15 strawberries, pass to the blender, we obtain a puree of strawberries
- 2 teaspoons of coconut sugar or agave syrup.

Cooking Direction:

1. In a bowl or pot with lid add the Chia seeds with the almond milk, mix with a fork.
2. Refrigerate for about eight hours (overnight).
3. Once the seeds of Chia are ready to be tasted, put your strawberries in a blender and mix to get a mashed texture.
4. Pour the strawberry puree on your Chia seeds
5. To assemble your breakfast, divide the pudding between 2 containers
6. Place the containers in the refrigerator

Storage, freeze, thaw and reheat guideline:

To store the pudding in the refrigerator, place it in containers and put the containers in the refrigerator at a temperature of about 40°F. When you want to heat your breakfast, all you have to do is to remove the waffles from the containers the heat the waffles in the waffle iron for 39 °F

Lunch: *Shrimp and broccoli paella*	
Preview: Prep Time: 7 min Cooking Time: 8 min Total Time: 15 min Serves: 2 Appliance: stove	**Nutrition per Serving:** Calories: 320; Fat: 168.5 g Carbs: 14 g, Protein 40 g Sugar: 3 g

Ingredients

- 4 2 bunch of broccoli
- 1 medium tomato
- 1 Celery stalk
- 1/2 medium zucchini
- 8 to 10 small shrimps
- 1 tablespoon of coconut fat
- 1 Tablespoon of almond butter
- 10 cl of coconut cream
- 1 small onion
- 1 teaspoon of basil
- 1 teaspoon of turmeric
- 1 pinch of cayenne pepper
- 1 pinch of salt
- 1 pinch of black pepper

Cooking Direction:

1. First, melt the coconut fat in a frying pan and fry the finely chopped onion or shallot over high heat until it starts to look translucent or even slightly brown. However, avoid burning it.
2. Then add the shrimp, and brown for a minute.
3. Then, incorporate one by one, the diced zucchini, the celery stalk, and the cabbage or broccoli into the mixture. And think of adding garlic, salt, before stirring everything. Then cover and stir every 2 minutes for 4 minutes.
4. Subsequently, add the tomato diced and cover. And let it melt in the mixture for 2 minutes. Then lower the heat again in half.
5. After that, melt the butter in the mixture while stirring. Then stop the fire. Finally, add the coconut cream, pepper, turmeric, chilli, and basil.

Storage, freeze, thaw and reheat guideline:

To store your lunch divide it in containers. Place the containers in the refrigerator at 39°F. When you want to heat your lunch, all you have to remove the containers from the refrigerator and reheat it in the microwave for about 3 minutes.

| 6. Finally, stir and let cool for 5 minutes
7. Now time to assemble the dish and to do that, divide your lunch into 2 containers and store it in the refrigerator | |

Soup: *Vegetable soup*

Preview:

Prep Time: 5 min
Cooking Time: 10 min
Total Time: 15 min
Serves: 2
Appliance: stove

Nutrition per Serving:

Calories: 230; Fat: 76.8 g
Carbs: 7 g, Protein 19.2 g
Sugar: 2 g

Ingredients

- ½ Pound of leeks
- ½ Pound of turnips
- 1 Celery branch
- 2 tablespoons of coconut oil
- 2 cups of liquid cream

Cooking Direction:

1. Detail all your vegetables and make them come back in a done with all the butter
2. Wet your vegetables a little higher than the level of these
3. Cook about 30 minutes covered
4. Mix your soup and add the cream, mix again
5. Divide your soup between two plastic containers and store it in the refrigerator for two days

Storage, freeze, thaw and reheat guideline:

To store this soup, divide it between two containers. Put the containers in the refrigerator at a temperature of 39°F. When you want to heat your lunch, all you have to do is to remove the containers from the refrigerator and reheat it in for about 5 minutes.

Snack: *Deviled eggs*

Preview:

Prep Time: 10 min
Cooking Time: 7 min
Total Time: 17 min
Serves: 2
Appliance: stove

Nutrition per Serving:

Calories: 145; Fat: 93 g
Carbs: 8 g, Protein 17 g
Sugar: 1.5 g

Ingredients

- 6 organic eggs
- 1/4 cup mayonnaise
- 2 teaspoons chopped fresh chives
- 1 tablespoon of avocado oil
- Paprika, to taste
- Finely sliced radishes for toppings
- 1 pinch of salt

Cooking Direction:

1. In a small saucepan, place the eggs and cover with cold water. Bring to a boil. When the water begins to boil, cover the pan and remove from heat. Let stand out of heat for 10 minutes.
2. Remove the eggs from the hot water and immerse them in very cold water to stop cooking.
3. Peel the eggs and cut it eggs in halves along the length and remove the yolks. Set aside.
4. In a bowl, with a fork, mash the egg yolks with the mayonnaise, avocado oil. Season with Salt and add the chives and mix gently.
5. Using two teaspoons stuff each half-egg with the filling and place on a serving platter.
6. Divide the eggs between two containers; then sprinkle each container with paprika and top with the radishes
7. Store the eggs in the refrigerator.

Storage, freeze, thaw and reheat guideline:

In order to store the devilled eggs; divide the eggs between two containers; then put the containers in the refrigerator at a temperature of 38°F. When you want to heat your snack, all you have to do is to remove the containers from the refrigerator and reheat the eggs in the microwave in for about 5 minutes.

Dinner : *Chicken and broccoli gratin*	
Preview: Prep Time: 10 min Cooking Time: 10 min Total Time: 20 min Serves: 2 Appliance: stove	**Nutrition per Serving:** Calories: 220; Fat: 113 g Carbs: 8 g, Protein 14 g Sugar: 1 g

Ingredients

- 1 pound of chicken breasts
- 14 cup of almond butter
- 100 cl of fresh cream
- 1 cup of goat cheese
- 2 organic eggs
- 2 Crushed garlic clove
- 1 pinch of salt
- 1 Pinch of pepper

Cooking Direction:

1. Cook the broccoli in a pot of water for 10 minutes. It must remain firm.
2. Melt the butter in a skillet; add the crushed garlic clove and the salted and peppered chicken. Let it get a brown color.
3. Drain the broccoli and mix with the chicken.
4. Beat the eggs with the cream, salt and pepper. Place broccoli and chicken in baking dish, cover with cream mixture and sprinkle with grated cheese.
5. Put in the oven at 390°F for 20 minutes.
6. When the gratin is ready; set it aside to cool for 3 minutes
7. Cut the gratin into two halves or in four portions
8. Place each two portions of gratin in a container so that you have two containers.

Storage, freeze, thaw and reheat guideline:

In order to store the gratin; divide the portions between two containers; then place the containers in the refrigerator at about temperature of 38°F. When you want to heat your dinner, all you have to do is to remove the containers from the refrigerator and reheat the gratin in the microwave in for about 4 minutes.

Meal Prep 6

The 12th, 13th and 14th day on keto diet

Meal Prep 6: The 12th; 13th and 14th day on keto diet		
Fresh Food Shopping List for 3 Days	**Meat and fish** 2 pounds of Chicken, Breast 1 pound of chicken, Legs 6 Bacon strips ½ pound of Ham Seafood Anchovy 1 pound of salmon 2 pounds of shrimp **Fats and oils** 3 cups of coconut oil 1 cup of olive oil 2 cups of almond butter	**Spices** Sea salt Black pepper Basil Cayenne pepper Cilantro Chili Powder Cinnamon Cumin Oregano Parsley Thyme Sage Rosemary Turmeric
	Vegetables 1 and ½ head of broccoli 1 head of cabbage 1 head of Cauliflower, raw 6 Celery stalks 5 Cucumbers 3 Eggplants 3 heads of garlic 1 Lettuce, Romaine 1 Bunch of Parsley 6 Radishes Spinach 5 Zucchinis 3 Carrots, raw Kale 4 onions **Fruits:** 1 pound of tomatoes 3 avocados 2 cups of Strawberries	**Dairy products** 3 Cups of Almond Milk (unsweetened) 3 cups coconut Cream 3 cups Coconut Milk (unsweetened) 1 Plain Greek Yogurt, whole milk 1 cup heavy Cream 12 eggs **Cheese** Cream Cheese 1 cup of mozzarella Cheese, whole milk Parmesan Cheese 2 cups of mozzarella cheese 2 cups goat cheese
Breakfast	Vanilla and chia smoothie	

Breakfast	Peach Cobbler
Lunch	Lettuce wraps with bacon
Soup	Broccoli and yogurt soup
Snack	Sausage dip
Dinner	Chicken Pizaiola
Nutrition intake per everyday:	Calories: 1561.2 | Fat: 298.3g | Carbohydrates: 24.5g | Protein 103.5 g | Sugar 11.9g

Breakfast: *Vanilla and chia smoothie*

Preview:

Prep Time: 5 min
Cooking Time: 5 min
Total Time: 10 min
Serves: 3
Appliance: stove

Nutrition per Serving:

Calories: 287; Fat: 68.5 g
Carbs: 6 g, Protein 8.7 g
Sugar: 2 g

Ingredients

- 3 tablespoons of diet Whey Vanilla
- 2 and ½ cups of organic soy milk
- 3 tbsp of ricotta
- 1 Cup of fresh raspberries
- 2 tablespoon walnuts
- 2 tablespoon of chia seeds

Cooking Direction:

1. In a blender, pour the soymilk.
2. Add the protein powder, ricotta, raspberries and nuts.
3. Mix until smooth and perfectly smooth
4. Transfer to a large glass and add the chia seeds.
5. Mix with a spatula to spread the chia.
6. Now divide the smoothie between 3 glass cans or containers and store it in the refrigerator

Storage, freeze, thaw and reheat guideline:

In order to store any smoothie in general, pour it in 3 glass containers; then place the containers in the refrigerator at a temperature of 40°F. When you want to heat your breakfast smoothie, all you have to do is to remove the containers from the refrigerator and wait a few minutes.

Breakfast: *Peach Cobbler*

Preview:

Prep Time: 10 min
Cooking Time: 40 min
Total Time: 10 min
Serves: 3
Appliance: oven

Nutrition per Serving:

Calories: 250; Fat: 52g
Carbs: 4.6 g, Protein 16 g
Sugar: 2.9 g

Ingredients

- 3 cups peaches peeled and chopped.
- 2 cups of almond flour
- ¼ cup of coconut flour
- 2 tablespoons of coconut oil
- ½ tablespoon of to baking soda
- 1 pinch of sea salt
- 1 cup of cream cheese
- 1 Tablespoon of raw honey
- 1/2 cup of softened ghee
- 3 drops of almond extract
- 3 tablespoons of Chia seeds
- 10 tablespoons of warm water
- 1 tablespoon of coconut vinegar

Cooking Direction:

1. Preheat the oven to 350 ° F, Grease an 8 by 8 pan with coconut oil. Pour the peaches in the pan.
2. Mix the almond flour, cream cheese, salt and baking soda in a bowl.
3. In a separate bowl, mix butter, honey and extract.
4. Combine the two mixtures.
5. In a small separate bowl, mix Chia seeds and warm water and let stand and thicken for 5 minutes.
6. After 5 minutes, add to the other mixtures.
7. Once well combined, add the vinegar and stir.
8. Pour the dough over the peaches, and cook for 30-45 minutes.
9. Once cooked, set the peach cobbler aside to cool for 5 minutes
10. Place the cobbler in 3 containers; then store the container in the refrigerator

Storage, freeze, thaw and reheat guideline:

In order to store the cobbler; place it in 3 containers; then place the containers in the refrigerator and store it at a temperature of 38°F. When you want to serve this breakfast, remove the containers from the refrigerator and microwave it for 5 minutes.

Lunch: *Lettuce wraps with bacon*

Preview:

Prep Time: 10 min
Cooking Time: 5 min
Total Time: 15 min
Serves: 3
Appliance: stove

Nutrition per Serving:

Calories: 278; Fat: 46g
Carbs: 4 g, Protein 15.8 g
Sugar: 1.5 g

Ingredients

- 1 lettuce iceberg head
- 4 slices of gluten free deli
- 2 slices of cooked gluten-free bacon
- 2 avocado, sliced
- 2 tomato, chopped

For Basil-Mayo:
- 1 cup gluten-free mayonnaise
- 6 large basil leaves, torn
- 1 teaspoon of lemon juice
- 2 clove of garlic, chopped
- 1 pinch salt
- 1 pinch pepper

Cooking Direction:

1. For basil-mayo: mix the ingredients in a small food processor and mix until smooth. Alternatively, chop basil and garlic and whisk all ingredients together. Can be done a few days per head of time.
2. Arrange three large lettuce leaves in the bottom of 3 containers
3. Coat each lettuce leaf with 1 slice of turkey and season with Basil-Mayo.
4. Place on a second slice of turkey followed by bacon, and a few slices of avocado and tomato.
5. Season lightly with salt and pepper, and then fold bottom up, sides in, roll like a burrito.
6. Store the containers in the refrigerator.

Storage, freeze, thaw and reheat guideline:

In order to store your lettuce wraps, place the containers in the refrigerator and set the temperature at about 39°F. When you want to serve your dish, remove from the refrigerator and set aside for a few minutes.

Soup: *Broccoli and yogurt soup*

Preview:

Prep Time: 5 min
Cooking Time: 5 min
Total Time: 10 min
Serves: 3
Appliance: Instant Pot

Nutrition per Serving:

Calories: 232; Fat: 52 g
Carbs: 3 g, Protein 14.6 g
Sugar: 1 g

Ingredients

- 2 tbsp of almond butter
- 5 shallots, coarsely chopped
- 1 sweet potato, cut into cubes
- 1/2 tablespoon of ground cumin
- 3 cloves of garlic, chopped
- 1 pinch salt and pepper
- 1 large broccoli, cut into large pieces
- 1 cup young spinach
- 1 tablespoon of maple syrup
- 4 cups vegetable broth
- 1/4 cup plain yogurt

Cooking Direction:

1. Preheat your Instant Pot by pressing the button saute; then melt the almond butter and soften the shallots for 3 to 4 minutes.
2. Add the sweet potato and cumin; continue cooking for about 3 minutes; then add the garlic.
3. Season with 1 pinch of salt
4. Add broccoli and spinach; then mix well so that broccoli soaks in spices and spinach has melted.
5. Add the maple syrup and cover with vegetable broth. Add water as needed. Lock the lid and seal the valve then cook for 15 minutes. When the timer beeps, remove the mixture from the instant pot

Storage, freeze, thaw and reheat guideline:

In order to store your soup, divide the soup between 3 containers and place the containers in the refrigerator and set the temperature at about 40°F. When you want to serve your soup, remove from the refrigerator

6. Mix with a blender with the yogurt. Adjust the seasoning; then serve with the accompaniment of your choice.
7. Divide the soup between 3 containers and store in the refrigerator. and reheat it in a pan for about 5 minutes.

Snack: *Sausage dip*

Preview:

Prep Time: 10 min
Cooking Time: 1 and ½ hours
Total Time: 10 minutes
Serves: 3
Appliance: Instant Pot

Nutrition per Serving:

Calories: 208.2; Fat: 45 g
Carbs: 4 g, Protein 12.4 g
Sugar: 3 g

Ingredients

- 1 lb spicy sausage, golden and drained
- ½ lb Velveeta style orange cheese, cubed
- 1 and ½ cups of sour cream
- ½ cup diced red onion
- 1 jalapeno, seeded and diced
- ½ cup of salsa
- ½ cup of milk
- ½ teaspoon of black pepper
- ½ teaspoon garlic powder

Cooking Direction:

1. Preheat your Instant pot to a temperature of 370° F; then add all the ingredients in your Instant Pot, starting with the solid ingredients.
2. Stir well. Cover and cook over high heat for 15 minutes
3. When the cheese is melted and the dip is hot, it is ready to serve.
4. Divide the dip between 3 containers and store it in the refrigerator for 3days

Storage, freeze, thaw and reheat guideline:

In order to store your dip, divide it between 3 plastic containers and place the 3 containers in the refrigerator and set the temperature at about 39°F. When you are ready to serve your soup; remove it from the refrigerator and place the dip containers over a pot of hot water.

Dinner: *Chicken Pizaiola*

Preview:

Prep Time: 10 min
Cooking Time: 20 min
Total Time: 30 min
Serves: 3
Appliance: Oven

Nutrition per Serving:

Calories: 306; Fat: 34.8 g
Carbs: 2.9 g, Protein 36g
Sugar: 1.5 g

Ingredients

- 3 chicken breasts
- 1 tray with ham
- 1 cup of pasta sauce
- 1 and ½ cups of grated cheese
- 1 Pinch of salt and pepper
- 2 Tablespoons of olive oil

Cooking Direction:

1. Preheat the oven to 290 °F
2. Place the 3 chicken breasts on a sheet of parchment paper directly on the plate of your oven.
3. Slice the breasts partially and garnish with sauce, ham and cheese.
4. Cover with grated cheese, season with salt and pepper and drizzle with oil.
5. Bake in a hot oven for 20 minutes
6. Once ready, divide the 2 chicken breasts between three containers
7. Seal the containers very well and store it in the refrigerator for 3 days

Storage, freeze, thaw and reheat guideline:

In order to store your dinner, the process is very easy; divide the chicken breasts between 3 containers. Put the containers in the refrigerator at a temperature of 40°F. When it is dinner time, remove the containers from the refrigerator and microwave the chicken for 5 minutes.

Meal Prep

7

The 15th and 16th days on keto diet

Meal Prep 7: The 15th and 16th days on keto diet

Fresh Food Shopping List for 2 Days	**Meat and fish** 5 cups of almond milk 3 cups of grated mozzarella 12 organic eggs 1 Greek yogurt 3 cups of cream cheese 3 cups of cheddar cheese 3 cups of mozzarella cheese **Nuts and seeds:** 1 cup of almonds 1 cup of nuts 1 cup sesame seeds 1 cup squash seeds ½ cup of flax seeds	**Vegetables:** 2 heads of cauliflower 3 avocados 1 lemon ½ pound of carrots 3 medium onions 5 zucchinis, 1 eggplant, 1 pound of fresh tomato, 3 Shallots 3 medium onions 4 cucumbers **Fruits** 4 Avocados 2 Cups of raspberry 2 Cups of strawberry 1 pound of tomato
	Dairy products: 3 dozen eggs ½ lb almond butter Thick cream ½ gallon of unsweetened almond milk 4 oz. grated parmesan cheese 8 oz packet pepper jack cheese slices 8 oz of sting cheese 8 oz of cream cheese Cheddar cheese	**Frozen products:** 10 oz. packet of frozen broccoli florets 10 oz. packet of frozen spinach **Flours** 4 cups of almond flour 3 cups Coconut flour **Spices** 2 Heads of garlic Salt Pepper Oregano Arugula

	8 oz of sour cream	ground cinnamon
	Grocery:	Pepper
	Salsa with sugar-free tomatoes	**Canned ingredients**
	1 cup unsweetened grated coconut	1 can of 8 oz of tomato sauce
		3 tablespoon of olive oil
		2 tablespoons of apple cider vinegar
	1 cup of dark chocolate with 85% cocoa	4 tablespoons sesame paste
		1 teaspoon of vanilla extract
	90 g dark chocolate with 85% cocoa to garnish	
Breakfast	Granola bars	
Appetizer	Stuffed cucumbers	
Lunch	Turkey curry	
Lunch	Salmon with capers	
Salad	Salmon and avocado salad	
Dinner	Cauliflower pizza	
Nutrition intake per day:	Calories: 1295.3| Fat: 377.5g	Carbohydrates: 29.6g	Protein 105.3 g	Sugar 11.4g	

Breakfast: *Granola bars*

Preview :
Prep Time: 10 min
Cooking Time: 18 min
Total Time: 28 min
Serves: 2
Appliance: Oven

Nutrition per Serving:
Calories: 230; Fat: 37.1g
Carbs: 3 g, Protein 12g
Sugar: 1.5 g

Ingredients

- 1 cup of almonds
- 1 cup of nuts
- 1 cup sesame seeds
- 1 cup squash seeds
- ½ cup of flax seeds
- 1 cup unsweetened grated coconut
- 1 cup of dark chocolate with 85% cocoa
- 6 tablespoons of coconut oil
- 4 tablespoons sesame paste
- 1 teaspoon of vanilla extract
- 2 teaspoons ground cinnamon
- 1 pinch of salt
- 2 organic eggs
- 90 g dark chocolate with 85% cocoa to garnish

Cooking Direction:

1. Preheat the oven to 350 °F.
2. Mix together (not too finely) all the ingredients.
3. Using a spatula spread the preparation in the mould (use a non stick pan or coated with baking paper).
4. Bake 15 to 20 minutes until the mixture turns a nice color but does not burn.
5. Let cook; then cut into about 20 to 24 bars.
6. Melt the topping chocolate in a microwave.
7. Dip each bar in melted chocolate halfway up and on one side only.
8. Cool completely.
9. Divide the bars between two containers
10. Store in the refrigerator or freezer

Storage, freeze, thaw and reheat guideline:
To store your granola and chocolate bars, make sure to arrange it carefully in 2 containers. Place the containers in the refrigerator at a temperature of about 39°F. When it is morning, remove the containers from the refrigerator microwave

Appetizer: *Stuffed cucumbers*

Preview:
Prep Time: 5 min
Cooking Time: 10 min
Total Time: 15 min
Serves: 2
Appliance: Oven

Nutrition per Serving:
Calories: 181; Fat: 33g
Carbs: 2.7 g, Protein 12 g
Sugar: 2 g

Ingredients

- 4 cucumbers
- ½ pound of cod or other white fish
- 2 organic eggs
- 1 lemon
- 1 Greek yogurt
- 1 Pinch salt and pepper

Cooking Direction:

1. Blanch the cucumbers in salted boiling water for 10 minutes.
2. Cut in half to dig them.
3. Cut the fish into pieces, mix with the eggs and yogurt, season; add the chopped cucumber flesh.
4. Stuff the cucumbers with this mixture and cook in the oven for 10 minutes on slices of lemon.
5. Once the time is up; turn the oven and set aside to cool
6. Divide the cucumbers between 2 containers and store in the refrigerator

Storage, freeze, thaw and reheat guideline:

In order to store the stuffed cucumbers; place every two cucumbers in 2 containers and make sure to arrange it carefully. Put the containers in the refrigerator at a temperature of about 40°F. To reheat this appetizer, steam it over a pot of hot water

Lunch : *Salmon with capers*

Preview :
Prep Time: 10 min
Cooking Time: 25 min
Total Time: 35 min
Serves: 2
Appliance: Stove and grill

Nutrition per Serving:
Calories: 283; Fat: 84g
Carbs: 6.5g, Protein 22 g
Sugar: 1 g

Ingredients

- 1 pound of salmon, cut
- ½ pound of sweet potatoes
- 1 sprig of thyme
- 1 clove of garlic
- 1 bay leaf
- 2 cups of cherry tomatoes
- 1 small shallot
- Salt and pepper
- ½ cup of olives
- 1 yellow lemon
- 1 tbsp of pine nuts
- 2 onions
- ½ bunch of chives
- 12 capers
- Dill
- 1 tbsp of olive oil

Cooking Direction:

1. Sprinkle the potatoes diced in a frying pan generously with oil.
2. Add thyme, garlic and bay leaves and cook over low heat for 20 to 25 minutes. Let them cool in the cooking oil.
3. Pour the drained potatoes into a pot-rack, add the tomatoes cut in four, chopped shallot and chives, thin sliced onions, raw lemon segments, golden walnuts and olives. Cover with olive oil and set aside at room temperature.
4. Season the salmon. Cook with a drizzle of olive oil over the grill.
5. Divide the salmon between 2 containers and add to it the sweet potatoes
6. Top with the capers and dill

Storage, freeze, thaw and reheat guideline:

In order to store your lunch, all you have to do is to divide it between 2 containers; then store it in the refrigerator at 38°F. To reheat this lunch, microwave it for about 4 or 5 minutes.

Lunch : *Turkey curry*

Preview :
Prep Time: 10 min
Cooking Time: 20 min
Total Time: 15 min
Serves: 2
Appliance: Oven

Nutrition per Serving:

Calories: 234; Fat: 74g
Carbs: 5.8g, Protein 22 g
Sugar: 2.4 g

Ingredients

- ½ pound of turkey stir-fried
- 1 tablespoon of sunflower oil,
- 2 zucchini,
- 1 eggplants,
- 1 tomato
- Salt and pepper,
- 2 cloves garlic,
- 2 shallots,
- 1 onion,
- 1 pepper

Cooking Direction:

1. Sauté the turkey chunks in a non-stick skillet with chopped onion and shallots.
2. When the meat is golden on all sides, cover with a little water and add a clove of garlic and the curry powder and simmer 20 minutes.
3. Season with salt and pepper, then add the zucchini cut into pieces, the peeled and diced eggplant and the tomato; peeled and seeded, and let reduce another 20 minutes over low heat.
4. The sauce should not be too runny

Storage, freeze, thaw and reheat guideline:
In order to store the turkey curry, it is very simple; all you have to do is to divide it between 2 containers; then store it in the refrigerator at 39°F. To reheat this lunch, microwave it for about 4 or 5 minutes.

Salad : *Salmon and avocado salad*	
Preview : Prep Time: 3 min Cooking Time: 5 min Total Time: 8 min Serves: 2 Appliance: stove	**Nutrition per Serving:** Calories: 131.3; Fat: 54 g Carbs: 4.6 g, Protein 12.5g Sugar: 1.5g

Ingredients

- 3 avocados
- 1 lemon
- ½ pound of marinated salmon
- 2 handfuls of arugula
- 3 tablespoon of olive oil
- 2 tablespoons of apple cider vinegar
- 1 tablespoon old-fashioned mustard 1 bunch of coriander or basil pepper

Cooking Direction:	**Storage, freeze, thaw and reheat guideline:**
1. Cut the avocados into halves and remove the stones, take the flesh with a spoon. 2. Arrange the balls in a bowl and sprinkle with the lemon juice. 3. Cut the marinated salmon into cubes, add them to the salad bowl with washed arugula and coriander or basil washed and chopped. 4. Mix oil, vinegar, mustard, salt, pepper and 2 tbsp. 5. Add a little bit of water and pour the sauce over the salad. 6. Stir gently and divide the salad between 2 containers 7. Store the containers in the refrigerator	In order to store this salad, you should first put it I a plastic wrap; then in a container and store it in the refrigerator at a temperature of 38°F. To reheat this salad, let it defrost for about 5 minutes before serving it.

Dinner : *Cauliflower pizza*

Preview :
Prep Time: 10 min
Cooking Time: 20 min
Total Time: 30 min
Serves: 2
Appliance: Oven

Nutrition per Serving:

Calories: 236; Fat: 95.4g
Carbs: 7 g, Protein 24.8g
Sugar: 3g

Ingredients

- 1 cauliflower
- ½ cup of grated mozzarella
- 1 organic egg
- 1 cup of white ham
- 1 cup of mozzarella
- 4 tbsp of tomato sauce
- ½ cup of grated cheese
- 1 teaspoon of oregano

Cooking Direction:

1. Cut the cauliflower head into small florets
2. Grate the cauliflower; the heat it for 4 minutes in the microwave
3. Fluff the cauliflower with a fork
4. Mix the egg and grated cheese with drained cauliflower until your obtain the dough
5. Spread the obtained mixture on a sheet of parchment paper and bake at 400°F until golden brown for about 15 to 20 minutes.
6. Garnish your pizza with olive and capers and
7. It's ready
8. Cut the pizza; then divide the portions between 2 containers and store it in the refrigerator for 2 days

Storage, freeze, thaw and reheat guideline:

In order to store your cauliflower pizza, arrange the portions between 2 containers and store the containers in the refrigerator. When you want to serve your pizza, remove the container from the fridge and microwave the pizza for about 4 minutes.

Meal Prep 8

The 17th and 18th days on keto diet

Meal Prep 8: The 17th and 18th days on keto diet

Fresh Food Shopping List for 2 Days

Meat and fish

- Sugar-free bacon
- Ground beef
- 1 roast chicken
- Sugar-free sausage
- 5-3lb. roasted boneless beef chuck

Frozen products:

- 6 oz of frozen broccoli florets
- 8 oz. packet of frozen spinach

Flours

- 1 Packet of gluten free Bruschetta bread
- 5 cups of almond flour
- 2 cups Coconut flour

Dairy products:

- 4 dozen eggs
- ½ lb almond butter
- Thick cream
- 1 gallon of unsweetened almond milk
- 8 oz of grated parmesan cheese
- 8 oz packet Philadelphia cheese
- 10 oz of cream cheese
- Grated Cheddar cheese
- 8 oz of mozzarella cheese

Produce:

- 1 Bunch of fresh spinach
- 1 Bunch of fresh basil
- 6 avocados
- An 8 oz packet of spinach leaves
- 2 cauliflowers
- 1 bunch of celery
- 1 red or yellow pepper
- 1 pound of tomato
- 5 small onions
- ½ pound of zucchini
- Fresh head of broccoli
- Chopped celery
- Sweet potatoes
- ½ pound of green beans

Grocery:

- 1 packet of protein flavouring chicken soup
- Light salt
- Cocoa powder
- 2 cups of chocolate chips
- 1 can of 5oz of drained tuna
- 2 tsp of balsamic vinegar

Spices

- 3 Heads of garlic
- Salt
- Pepper

Breakfast	Cocoa chocolate shake
Lunch	Chuck roast
Soup	Spinach and onion soup
Snack	Stuffed tomatoes
Dinner	Ketogenic low carb Cloud Bread
Dinner	Ketogenic Bruschetta
Nutrition intake per day:	Calories: 1278	Fat: 130g	Carbohydrates: 24.5g	Protein 107 g	Sugar 12.8g

Breakfast: *Cocoa chocolate shake*

Preview:
Prep Time: 10 min
Cooking Time: 15 min
Total Time: 25 min
Serves: 3
Appliance: blender

Nutrition per Serving:
Calories: 236; Fat: 26g
Carbs: 5 g, Protein 26g
Sugar: 2.3g

Ingredients

- 1 cup of unsweetened almond milk
- 1 cup of ice
- 2 tablespoons of cocoa powder
- ½ cup of chocolate chips
- 1/2 cup of raw spinach
- 1/2 cup of fresh raspberries
- 1 and ½ tablespoons of almond butter

Cooking Direction:

1. Melt the chocolate in a microwave safe bowl with the almond butter
2. Place the almond milk with the ice, the chocolate in a blender
3. Add the spinach, and the raspberries in blender and cover.
4. Blend your ingredients until it becomes smooth.
5. Divide the shake in 3 glass containers
6. Store the shake in the refrigerator.

Storage, freeze, thaw and reheat guideline:

In order to store your shake, pour it in glass containers and seal it very well. Store the containers in the refrigerator at a temperature of about 40°F. When you serve your shake, remove the containers from the refrigerator and set it aside for 10 minutes;

Lunch : *Chuck roast with balsamic vinegar*

Preview :
Prep Time: 5 min
Cooking Time: 35 min
Total Time: 40 min
Serves: 3
Appliance: blender

Nutrition per Serving:
Calories: 342; Fat: 48g
Carbs: 5 g, Protein 30g
Sugar: 5g

Ingredients

- A boneless roast of chuck, about 3 pounds.
- 1 C. Kosher salt soup
- 1 teaspoon black ground pepper
- 1 teaspoon of garlic powder
- 1/4 cup of balsamic vinegar
- 2 cups of water
- 1/2 cup chopped onion
- 1/4 teaspoon of xanthan
- Fresh parsley, chopped to garnish

Cooking Direction:

1. Cut the chuck roast in halves. Season the roast with 1 pinch of salt, pepper and 1 pinch of garlic powder on all sides. Using the setting functions on the instant pot, brown the roast pieces on both sides.
2. Add 1/4 cup of balsamic vinegar, 1 cup of water and 1/2 cup of onion to the meat. Cover and seal, then using the manual button set the timer for 35 minutes. When the timer beeps, release the pressure by moving the lever to the "ventilation" setting. Once all the pressure is released discover the pot.
3. Gently remove the meat from the pan in a large bowl. Break down thoroughly and remove any large pieces of grease or other waste.
4. Use the function setting to boil and leave remaining liquid in the pot and simmer for 10 minutes to reduce.
5. Stir in the xanthan gum while whisking, then add the meat to the pan and stir gently.

Storage, freeze, thaw and reheat guideline:

In order to store your lunch, place it in 3 containers and store the containers in the refrigerator at a temperature of about 38°F. When you serve your chuck roast, remove the containers from the refrigerator and reheat it in the oven for about 5 minutes.

6. Turn off your instant pot and slice the chuck roast into slices; then divide the slices into plastic containers and store it in the refrigerator for 3 days.	

Stew: *Spinach and onion stew*

Preview:
Prep Time: 5 min
Cooking Time: 5 min
Total Time: 10 min
Serves: 3
Appliance: Instant Pot

Nutrition per Serving:
Calories: 270; Fat: 17g
Carbs: 6 g, Protein 11g
Sugar: 1g

Ingredients

- 1 packet of protein flavouring chicken soup
- 2 and ½ cups of coconut milk
- 1 small onion, chopped
- 1 whole organic egg
- 1 shallot
- some green beans already cooked
- 1/2 zucchini

Cooking Direction:

1. Preheat your Instant pot to a temperature of 380° F
2. Lightly sauté the onion and garlic in an oiled saucepan for 5 minutes.
3. Add the spinach and stir until they are all reduced.
4. Pour the water or broth, salt lightly and lock the lid; then cook for 10 minutes.
5. Stir the stew very well. Pour the coconut milk.
6. Stir again, season very well
7. Divide the stew between 2 containers and add the nut

Storage, freeze, thaw and reheat guideline:

In order to store your stew, place it in 3 containers and store it in the refrigerator at a temperature of 40 °F. When you serve your soup, just remove the containers from the refrigerator and reheat it in a pan for about 5 minutes

Snack : *Stuffed tomatoes*

Preview :
Prep Time: 5 min
Cooking Time: 8 min
Total Time: 13 min
Serves: 3
Appliance: Oven

Nutrition per Serving:
Calories: 180; Fat: 12 g
Carbs: 3 g, Protein 23g
Sugar: 0.5g

Ingredients

- 3 medium tomatoes
- 1 can of 5oz of drained tuna
- 2 tsp of balsamic vinegar
- 1 Tablespoon of chopped green onion
- 1 Tablespoon/ ¼ oz of chopped mozzarella
- 1 Tablespoon of chopped fresh basil

Cooking Direction:

- Cut the top of the tomato; then scoop the inside of a spoon with a spoon; then set it aside
- Make the tuna filling by stirring all together the tuna with the balsamic vinegar, the mozzarella, the basil, and the green onion.
- Fill the tomatoes with the tuna filling
- Arrange the tomatoes in a greased baking tray
- Top the tomatoes with the cheese
- Bake the tomatoes in an oven for about 8 minutes at a temperature of 360° F
- Once the tomatoes are cooked, divide it between 3 containers
- Lock the containers and store it in the refrigerator for 3 days

Storage, freeze, thaw and reheat guideline:

In order to store your snack, place it in 3 containers and store it in the refrigerator at a temperature of 38°F. When you serve your soup, just remove the containers from the refrigerator and reheat it in a microwave for about 5 minutes

Dinner: *Ketogenic low carb Cloud Bread*

Preview:
Prep Time: 10 min
Cooking Time: 15 min
Total Time: 25 min
Serves: 3
Appliance: Oven

Nutrition per Serving:
Calories: 97; Fat: 17g
Carbs: 2 g, Protein 10g
Sugar: 3g

Ingredients

- 1 teaspoon of baking powder
- 1 Cup of Philadelphia cheese
- 3 Organic egg

Cooking Direction:

1. Separate the whites from the yolks of the three eggs. Place the whites in one bowl and the yolks in the other.
2. Add the cheese at room temperature to the yolks and mix with an electric mixer to obtain a fine paste.
3. Add the baking soda to the egg whites and mix with the mixer.
4. Mix both mixtures gently with a spatula.
5. Preheat the oven to 300°F. Spread small circles of dough on parchment paper.
6. Cook for 15 to 20 minutes.
7. Once the cloud bread is cooked, set it aside to cool for about 5 minutes
8. Divide the cloud bread between 3 plastic wraps; then plastic the plastic wraps in two containers
9. Store the containers in the refrigerator for 3 days

Storage, freeze, thaw and reheat guideline:

In order to store your Ketogenic cloud breads, put the bread in 3 containers in the refrigerator at a temperature of about 39°F. When you serve your dinner; remove the containers from the refrigerator and remove the bread clouds from the plastic wraps; then microwave it for about 5 minutes.

Dinner : *Ketogenic Bruschetta*

Preview :
Prep Time: 10 min
Cooking Time: 45 min
Total Time: 55min
Serves: 3
Appliance: Oven

Nutrition per Serving:

Calories: 153; Fat: 10g
Carbs: 3.5 g, Protein 7g
Sugar: 1g

Ingredients

- 1 teaspoon of baking powder
- 1 Cup of Philadelphia cheese
- 3 Organic egg
- 1 and ½ cups of black olives
- 1 capers
- 24 cherry tomatoes
- oregano
- olive oil
- 1 clove of garlic

Cooking Direction:

1. Wash, dry and put the peppers on a baking sheet covered with parchment paper.
2. Bake at 400° F for one hour, turning over on the other side after 30 minutes.
3. Put the roasted peppers in a food bag for 15 minutes.
4. Clean the peppers removing the skin and seeds.
5. Put the peppers on a plate and season with olive oil
6. Wash, dry and halve the cherry tomatoes.
7. Heat a peel and roast the tomatoes on both sides.
8. Toss the slices of Pan Bruschetta so that they are crunchy on the outside.
9. Rub the clove of garlic on the slices of bread.
10. Put the pitted olives in the bowl of a blender and mash them.
11. Coat the slices with olive puree, then cover with peppers cut in fillets, add the tomatoes, some capers, sprinkle with oregano and drizzle with a little olive oil

Storage, freeze, thaw and reheat guideline:

In order to store your Ketogenic Bruschetta, divide it between 3 containers and place the containers in the refrigerator at a temperature of 40°F.When you want to serve your dinner, remove the containers from the refrigerator and microwave the Bruschetta for about 4 minutes.

Meal Prep

9

The 19th, 20th and 21st days on keto diet

Meal prep 9: The 19th, 20th and 21st days on keto diet			
Fresh Food Shopping List for 3 Days	**Meat and fish** 1 pound of ground pork 2 pounds of ground beef ¼ pound of ground beef liver 2 Large cauliflower florets 5 sheets of square nori (algae wraps) 10 oz cooked salmon or canned salmon		**Produce:** 1 Bunch of fresh basil 6 avocados An 10 oz packet of spinach leaves 3 cauliflowers 1 bunch of celery 2 packages of romaine lettuce hearts 1 red or yellow pepper 2 tomatoes 4 Granny smith apples
	Dairy products: 3 dozen eggs ½ lb almond butter Thick cream ½ gallon of unsweetened almond milk 4 oz. grated parmesan cheese 8 oz packet pepper jack cheese slices 8 oz of sting cheese 8 oz of cream cheese Cheddar cheese 8 oz of sour cream		**Frozen products:** 10 oz. packet of frozen broccoli florets 10 oz. packet of frozen spinach **Grocery:** Salsa with sugar-free tomatoes 1 tablespoon of maple syrup Dried sage **Spices** 2 Heads of garlic Salt

	Flours 4 cups of almond flour 3 cups Coconut flour 2 cups Coconut Aminos	Pepper Ginger Dried sage
Breakfast a	Liver and beef patties with eggs	
Appetizer b	Cauliflower fritters	
Lunch c	Ketogenic Sushi	
Lunch d	Pork chops with apples	
Snack e	Pineapples with bacon wraps	
Salad :	Salmon salad with red onions and granny smith apples	
Nutrition intake per day:	Calories: 1550	Fat: 141.2g	Carbohydrates: 20.3g	Protein 96 g	Sugar 9.1g	

Breakfast: *Liver and beef patties with eggs*

Preview:
Prep Time: 10 min
Cooking Time: 10 min
Total Time: 20 min
Serves: 3
Appliance: Oven

Nutrition per Serving:
Calories: 349; Fat: 28g
Carbs: 1.5 g, Protein 15g
Sugar: 1.9g

Ingredients

- ¾ pound of ground pork
- ½ pound of ground beef
- ¼ pound of ground beef liver
- 1 tablespoon of maple syrup
- 1 teaspoon of dried sage
- ½ teaspoon of dried thyme
- ½ teaspoon of dried rosemary
- ½ teaspoon of sea salt
- ½ teaspoon of black pepper
- 2 tablespoon of olive oil
- 4 large organic egg

Cooking Direction:

1. Combine the pork meat with the beef, the liver, the maple syrup, the seasonings, 1 pinch of salt and 1 pinch of pepper in a bowl.
2. Mix the ingredients with both your hands until everything is perfectly combined
3. Form patties from the mixture of the meat
4. Heat half the quantity of the olive oil in a large skillet and cook your patties until it gets a golden brown color
5. Remove the sausages from the oil and add the remaining quantity of oil
6. Fry the eggs to your likings
7. Divide the sausages and the eggs between 3 containers and add the eggs to the containers too
8. Store the containers in the refrigerator for 3 days

Storage, freeze, thaw and reheat guideline:

In order to store your liver patties, divide it between 3 containers and place the containers in the refrigerator at a temperature of 39°F. When you want to serve your breakfast, remove the containers from the refrigerator and set the patties aside to room temperature for 10 minutes; then microwave it for about 3 minutes

Appetizer : *Cauliflower fritters*

Preview :
Prep Time: 10 min
Cooking Time: 10 min
Total Time: 20 min
Serves: 2
Appliance: Stove

Nutrition per Serving:

Calories: 205; Fat: 26g
Carbs: 4 g, Protein 13g
Sugar: 2.4g

Ingredients

- 1 large cauliflower head; cut into small florets
- 2 large eggs
- 1 cup of cream cheese
- 2/3 cup of almond flour
- 1 tablespoon of nutritional yeast
- ½ teaspoon of turmeric
- ½ teaspoon of sea salt
- ¼ teaspoon of black pepper
- 1-2 tablespoon of ghee
- 2 tablespoons of avocado oil

Cooking Direction:

1. Add the cauliflower florets to a large pot filled with water. Bring the cauliflower to a boil and let it boil for about 8 minutes. Strain the cauliflower.
2. Add in the florets in a food processor and pulse it until it is riced.
3. Add the cauliflower, the ghee, the cream cheese, the eggs, the almond flour, the nutritional yeast, the turmeric, the salt and the pepper to a large mixing bowl. Stir very well to combine; then form into medium patties.
4. Now, heat the ghee over a medium high heat in a large skillet.
5. Scoop half of the obtained mixture in around three fritters and cook it until it gets a golden brown color over each side for about 3 to 4 minutes.
6. Set the rest of the fritters aside and cook the rest
7. Divide the fritters between 3 containers and set store it in the refrigerator for 3 days

Storage, freeze, thaw and reheat guideline:

To store your appetizer, it is very simple, all you have to do is to divide the fritters between 3 containers and place it in the refrigerator at a temperature of 38°F. When you want to serve your appetizer, remove the containers from the refrigerator and set the fritters aside; then microwave it for about 4 minutes

Lunch: *Ketogenic Sushi*

Preview:
Prep Time: 10 min
Cooking Time: 5 min
Total Time: 15 min
Serves: 3
Appliance: Not cooked

Nutrition per Serving:
Calories: 335; Fat: 19.7g
Carbs: 2.3 g, Protein 12g
Sugar: 2g

Ingredients

- 3 sheets of square nori (algae wraps)
- 5-6 oz cooked salmon or canned salmon
- ⅓ red pepper, cut into thin strips
- ½ avocado, cut into strips
- ½ small cucumber, cut into strips
- 2 tablespoons of coconut oil
- 1 scallion / shallot cut into 2 to 3" pieces
- 2 tablespoons of mayonnaise
- 2 tablespoons of goat cheese
- 1 tablespoon of hot sauce or Sriracha sauce
- 1 teaspoon of black or white sesame seeds
- Coconut Aminos for dipping

Cooking Direction:

1. Place the nori leaf on a flat surface, such as a cutting board, shiny side down. Look at the fibres of the package to see which side to roll on.
2. Add one-third of the salmon to the right or left third of the nori leaf and garnish with two strips of pepper, cucumber and avocado. Add a little bit of green onion, the mayonnaise and spicy sauce. You can sprinkle with sesame seeds now or at a later stage once the rolls are cut.
3. Lightly wet the top of the nori sheet (the side you roll towards), just 1-2 cm from the package.
4. Take the opposite outer edge part of the roll and start wrapping it on the ingredients, using your fingers to keep it well and tight. Roll it until the top edge of the wrapper overlaps the roll and press firmly to glue it.
5. Place the roll on the cutting board with the seam facing down, and then cut into bite-size pieces.
6. Pack in 3 containers for lunch in the fridge for 3 days

Storage, freeze, thaw and reheat guideline:

In order to store your sushi, divide it between 3 containers and place the containers in the refrigerator at a temperature of 38°F. When you want to serve your lunch, remove the containers from the refrigerator and set the sushi aside to room temperature for 10 minutes; then serve

Lunch: *Pork chops with apples*

Preview:
Prep Time: 5 min
Cooking Time: 40 min
Total Time: 45 min
Serves: 3
Appliance: Not cooked

Nutrition per Serving:
Calories: 358; Fat: 27g
Carbs: 6 g, Protein 38g
Sugar: 1.5g

Ingredients

- 2 tablespoons of ghee
- 1 and 1/2 tablespoons of coconut oil
- ½ Teaspoon of sea salt
- 4 Boneless pork chops in ½ inch each
- 2 tbsp of monk fruit sweetener
- 1 tsp of cinnamon
- 1/8 tsp of nutmeg
- 1 tbsp of apple cider vinegar

Cooking Direction:

1. Melt the ghee and the coconut oil in a large skillet over a medium heat, add the pork chops and cook for about 5 minutes.
2. Flip the pork chops; then add in the chayote and sprinkle the sweetener, the cinnamon, the nutmeg, and the apple cider vinegar over the top of the chops.
3. Cook for about 5 more minutes; then remove the pork chops from the skillet and place it in 2 containers
4. Place the chayote mixture in a pan and let boil for a few minutes
5. Bring the chayote mixture to a boil for several minutes. Reduce the heat to a low medium and let simmer with a cover on for about 30 minutes
6. Divide the chayote apples between the 3 containers with the pork chops
7. Store the containers in the refrigerator

Storage, freeze, thaw and reheat guideline:

In order to store your lunch, divide it between 3 containers and place the containers in the refrigerator at a temperature of 39°F. When you want to serve your lunch, remove the containers from the refrigerator and set microwave it for 5 minutes; then serve

Snack: *Pineapples with bacon*

Preview:
Prep Time: 5 min
Cooking Time: 20 min
Total Time: 25 min
Serves: 3
Appliance: Not cooked

Nutrition per Serving:
Calories: 163; Fat: 27g
Carbs: 4 g, Protein 10g
Sugar: 2g

Ingredients

- 12 strips of bacon
- 24 2-inch of pineapple cubes
- 2 tablespoons of avocado oil
- 1 tablespoons of coconut oil
- 2 Tablespoons of pure maple syrup
- 2 teaspoons of spicy brown mustard

Cooking Direction:

1. Preheat the oven of a temperature of 400°F.
2. Line a baking sheet with a parchment paper.
3. Cut the bacon strips in two halves.
4. Wrap each of the pineapple cubes with a bacon slice and lay it over a bacon sheet with the seam down
5. Melt the coconut oil
6. Whisk mustard with the maple syrup, the melted coconut oil and avocado oil until the ingredients are very well combined
7. Brush each of the pineapple cubes with the maple mustard.
8. Spear each of the cubes with a toothpick.
9. Bake the bacon wrapped pineapples for about 15 to 20 minutes, until it gets a golden brown color and crispy texture.
10. Divide the bacon wrapped pineapples between 3 containers and store in the refrigerator

Storage, freeze, thaw and reheat guideline:

In order to store your snack, divide it between 3 containers and place the containers in the refrigerator at a temperature of 40°F. When you want to serve your snack, remove the containers from the refrigerator and set it aside for 10 minutes; then serve

Salad : *Salmon salad with red onions and granny smith apples*

Preview :
Prep Time: 2 hours min
Cooking Time: 5 min
Total Time: 2 hours and 5 min
Serves: 3
Appliance: Not cooked

Nutrition per Serving:
Calories: 140; Fat: 23.5g
Carbs: 2.5 g, Protein 8g
Sugar: 1.2g

Ingredients

- 1 Pound of fresh salmon fillet
- 2 Large granny smith apples
- 3 tablespoons of goat cheese
- 1 tablespoon of cream cheese
- 2 small red onions
- 3 small limes
- 2 tablespoons of olive oil

Cooking Direction:

1. Cut the fresh fish in small cubes or thin slices. Put them in a dish. Sprinkle with olive oil. Add the cream cheese and goat cheese. Add salt.
2. Peel the onions and cut them into thin slices. Add them to the dish.
3. Clean the apples, remove the stumps, and cut them into medium quarters. Add them to the dish.
4. Squeeze the limes and sprinkle the dish with. Make sure the apple pieces are well watered so they do not oxidize before tasting.
5. Marinate in a cool place for 2 hours.
6. Divide your ingredients in 3 containers and store in the refrigerator

Storage, freeze, thaw and reheat guideline:

In order to store your salad, divide the salad between 3 containers and place it in the refrigerator at a temperature of about 39°F. When you are ready to serve your salad, remove the containers from the refrigerator and set it aside for 5 minutes; then serve

Meal Prep 10

The 22nd and 23rd days on keto diet

	Meal prep 10: The 22nd and 23rd days on keto diet	
Fresh Food Shopping List for 2 Days	**Meat and fish**	**Produce:**
	½ Pound of sugar-free bacon	1 Bunch of fresh basil
	2 Pounds of ground beef	8 avocados
	1 Pound of liver	8 oz packet of spinach leaves
	1 roast chicken	2 Heads of cauliflower
	2 Pounds of shrimp	1 bunch of celery
	Sugar-free sausage	1 red or yellow pepper
	5-3lb. roasted boneless beef chuck	2 tomatoes
		2 Pounds of eggplants
	1 Pound of ahi Tuna	Toasted pine nuts
	Dairy products:	**Frozen products:**
	4 dozen eggs	8 oz. packet of frozen broccoli florets
	1 Cup of almond butter	9 oz. packet of frozen spinach
	Thick cream	Parsley
	½ gallon of unsweetened almond milk	**Grocery:**
	8 oz. grated parmesan cheese	Light salt
	8 oz mozzarella cheese slices	Salsa with sugar-free tomatoes
	8 oz of sting cheese	**Flours**
	8 oz of cream cheese	4 cups of almond flour
	Cheddar cheese	3 cups Coconut flour **Spices**
	8 oz of sour cream	3 Heads of garlic
	9 oz of mayonnaise	Salt

		Pepper
		Ginger
		Other ingredients
		Mustard
Breakfast a	Avocado, almond milk smoothie
Lunch b	Eggplant sandwiches
Snack c	Scottish eggs
Dinner d	Ahi tuna bowl
Dinner e	Stuffed Spinach and beef burgers
Salad f	Shrimp salad with avocado and lemon
Nutrition intake per day:	Calories: 1599 | Fat: 153.5g | Carbohydrates: 27.1g | Protein 73.8 g | Sugar 11.2g

Breakfast: *Avocado, almond milk smoothie*

Preview:
Prep Time: 5 min
Cooking Time: 5 min
Total Time: 10 min
Serves: 2
Appliance: Blender

Nutrition per Serving:
Calories: 173; Fat: 14 g
Carbs: 3 g, Protein 12 g
Sugar: 2.2g

Ingredients

- 3 to 4 oz of avocado
- 3/4 cup of full - fat coconut milk
- ¼ cup of almond milk
- 1 tsp of fresh grated ginger
- 1/2 tsp of turmeric
- 1 tsp of lemon or of lime juice
- 1 cup of crushed ice
- 1 teaspoon of sugar-free sweetener to taste

Cooking Direction:

1. Add the first set of about 6 ingredients to a food processor or a blender over a low-speed until the mixture becomes smooth.
2. Add the crushed ice and the sweetener. Blend over a high speed until it becomes smooth.
3. Taste your smoothie and adjust the sweetness and the taste to your buds
4. Divide the smoothie into 2 containers and store it in the refrigerator for 2 days

Storage, freeze, thaw and reheat guideline:

To store your smoothie, divide it between two containers and store it in the refrigerator in the airtight containers at a temperature of 39°F.

Lunch: *Eggplant sandwiches*

Preview:
Prep Time: 5 min
Cooking Time: 10 min
Total Time: 15 min
Serves: 2
Appliance: Panini press

Nutrition per Serving:
Calories: 235; Fat: 26 g
Carbs: 3.5 g, Protein 10 g
Sugar: 3g

Ingredients

- 2 Small Eggplants with the ends removed
- 2 peeled garlic cloves
- 2 tbsp of Mayonnaise
- 1/2 cup of cream cheese
- 8-10 chopped lemon Basil leaves
- 1/2 cup of shredded Mozzarella
- 1/4 cup of goat cheese
- 2 tablespoons of avocado oil
- 2 small tomatoes
- 1 cup of spinach Leaves
- 2 tbsp of toasted Pine Nuts

Cooking Direction:

- Heat a Panini machine press to a medium heat.
- Remove the ends of each baby eggplant and slice it in halves; then cut it to the end to end.
- Slice the rest of the eggplant into pieces of ½ inch each and discard any skinny pieces.
- In a large and hot skillet, heat the avocado oil, brown the garlic cloves until it becomes fragrant and smooth. Once it becomes cool, mince the garlic and add it to the mayonnaise, the goat cheese and the cream cheese.
- Stir in the chopped lemon basil to finish the eggplant sandwiches
- Divide the sandwiches between 2 airtight containers; then store it in the refrigerator

Storage, freeze, thaw and reheat guideline:

To store your lunch, divide the lunch between 2 containers and store it in the refrigerator for 2 days at a temperature of 38°F

Snack : *Scottish eggs*	
Preview : Prep Time: 5 min Cooking Time: 5 min Total Time: 10 min Serves: 2 Appliance: Stove	**Nutrition per Serving:** Calories: 256; Fat: 38 g Carbs: 4 g, Protein 20 g Sugar: 2.1g

Ingredients

- 4 organic eggs
- ½ Pound of sausage meat
- 1 Small white onion
- 1 Finely chopped garlic clove
- 1 tablespoon of mustard
- 2 tablespoons of cream cheese
- 1 pinch of salt
- 1 pinch of pepper
- 2 tablespoons of almond flour
- 2 organic beaten eggs
- 1 tablespoon of avocado oil

Cooking Direction:	**Storage, freeze, thaw and reheat guideline:**
1. Cook the eggs for 8 minutes in boiling water, in order to have boiled eggs. 2. Mix sausage meat with finely chopped onion, chopped garlic, the cream cheese, the avocado oil and mustard. Salt and pepper. When the eggs are cooked, peel them. 3. Take 1 quarter of the meat mixture, and flatten it in the hand. 4. Roll an egg in the flour, and place it on the flattened meat. Wrap the meat around the egg. Dredge the obtained balls in the beaten eggs, then in the almond flour 5. Fry for about 5 minutes. 6. Divide the Scottish eggs between 2 containers and store in the refrigerator for 2 days	To store your snack, divide the scotch eggs between 2 containers and store it in the refrigerator for 2 days at a temperature of 40°F

Dinner : *Ahi tuna bowl*

Preview :
Prep Time: 10 min
Cooking Time: 5 min
Total Time: 15 min
Serves: 2
Appliance: Stove

Nutrition per Serving:
Calories: 248; Fat: 16.5 g
Carbs: 3.6 g, Protein 9.8 g
Sugar: 1.4g

Ingredients

- 1 lb of diced ahi tuna, chopped
- 1 tbsp of coconut Aminos
- ½ tsp of sesame oil
- 1/4 cup of mayonnaise
- 2 tablespoons of cream cheese
- 2 Tablespoons of sriracha
- 1 Diced, ripe avocado
- 1/2 cup of Kimchi
- ½ Cup of chopped green onion
- 1 tablespoon of avocado oil
- 1 pinch of sesame seeds

Cooking Direction:

1. Add the avocado oil to the bowl; then add the diced tuna.
2. Add the coconut aminos, the cream cheese, the sesame oil, the mayo, the sriracha to the bowl and toss it very well to combine.
3. Add the diced avocado and the kimchi to the bowl and combine it very well.
4. Divide the Kimchi between two containers; then add the greens, the cauliflower rice and the chopped green onion with the sesame seeds
5. Store the containers in the refrigerator for 2 days.

Storage, freeze, thaw and reheat guideline:

In order to store your dinner, make sure to divide it between 2 containers. Put the containers in the refrigerator at a temperature of about 40°F. When you want to serve your dinner, remove the containers from the refrigerator and microwave for a few minutes.

Dinner: *Stuffed Spinach and beef burgers*

Preview:
Prep Time: 5 min
Cooking Time: 8 min
Total Time: 13 min
Serves: 2
Appliance: Griller

Nutrition per Serving:
Calories: 400; Fat: 27 g
Carbs: 4 g, Protein 22 g
Sugar: 1.9g

Ingredients

- 1 lb of ground chuck roast
- 1 teaspoon of salt
- ¾ teaspoon of ground black pepper
- 2 tablespoons of cream cheese
- 1 tablespoon of avocado oil
- 1 cup of firmly packed fresh spinach
- ½ cup of shredded mozzarella cheese (4 to 5 oz)
- 2 tablespoons of grated Parmesan cheese

Cooking Direction:
1. In a large bowl, combine the ground beef with the salt, and the pepper.
2. Scoop about ⅓ cup of the mixture and with wet hands; shape about 4 patties about ½-inch of thickness. Place the patties in the refrigerator.
3. Place the spinach in a saucepan over a medium-high heat.
4. Cover the pan and cook for about 2 minutes, until the spinach becomes wilted.
5. Drain the spinach and let cool; then squeeze the spinach
6. Cut the spinach and put it in a bowl; then stir in the mozzarella cheese, the cream cheese, the avocado oil and the Parmesan.
7. Scoop ¼ cup of the stuffing and shape 4 patties; then cover with the remaining 4 patties
8. Seal both the edges of each burger
9. Cup each of the patties with your hands to make it round

Storage, freeze, thaw and reheat guideline:

In order to store your dinner, make sure to divide it between 2 containers. Place the containers in the refrigerator at a temperature of about 39°F. When you want to serve your dinner, remove the containers from the refrigerator and microwave for 5 minutes.

10. Press each of the patties a little bit to make a thick layer Heat your grilling pan over a high heat
11. Grill your burgers for about 6 minutes on each of the two sides.
12. Divide the burgers between 2 containers
13. Store in the refrigerator Serve!

Salad : *Shrimp Salad*	
Preview : Prep Time: 5 min Cooking Time: 30 min Total Time: 35 min Serves: 2 Appliance: Not cooked	**Nutrition per Serving:** Calories: 287; Fat: 32g Carbs: 9 g, Protein 22g Sugar: 0.3g

Ingredients

- 1 Pound of cooked shelled shrimps
- 2 avocados
- 2 lemons
- 2 tablespoons of avocado oil
- 1 onion
- 1 bunch of parsley
- 2 tablespoons of cream cheese
- salt and pepper

Cooking Direction:	**Storage, freeze, thaw and reheat guideline:**
1. Squeeze the lemons and pour the juice into a bowl. 2. Peel and chop the onion. Add it to the lemon juice. 3. Marinate shrimp in lemon juice for 1/2 hour. 4. Peel and stone the avocados; then cut the flesh into cubes. Add them to the salad bowl. 5. Chop the parsley and add 1 pinch of salt, 1 pinch of pepper and mix the cream cheese with avocado oil and mix the whole thing. 6. Divide the salad in 2 containers 7. Store the salad in the refrigerator	In order to store your salad, make sure to divide it between 2 containers. Place the containers in the refrigerator at a temperature of about 40°F. When you want to serve your salad, remove the containers from the refrigerator and set it aside for 5 minutes then serve it

Meal Prep 11

The 24th and 25th days on keto diet

Meal Prep 11: The 24th and 25th days on keto diet			
Fresh Food Shopping List for 2 Days	**Meat and fish**		**Produce:**
	Sugar-free bacon		Bunch of fresh basil
	Ground beef		3 avocados
	2 Pounds of chicken breasts		An 4oz packet of spinach leaves
	Sugar-free sausage		1 cauliflower head
	5-3lb. roasted boneless beef chuck		1 bunch of celery
			1 red or yellow pepper
	1 Pound of salmon		1 Pound of tomato
	1 Pound of ground beef		3 Cucumbers
			6 cups of green olives
	Dairy products:		**Frozen products:**
	1 dozen eggs		10 oz. packet of frozen broccoli florets
	1 Cup of coconut oil		10 oz. packet of frozen spinach
	Thick cream		
	½ gallon of unsweetened almond milk		2 Cups of Worcestershire sauce
	4 oz. grated parmesan cheese		**Grocery:**
	8 oz packet pepper jack cheese slices		Light salt
			Salsa with sugar-free tomatoes
	8 oz of sting cheese		**Spices**
	8 oz of cream cheese		2 Heads of garlic
	Cheddar cheese		Salt
	8 oz of sour cream		Pepper

Breakfast	Almond flour Bread
Appetizer	Salmon rolls with cucumber
Lunch	Ketogenic chicken skillet
Dinner	Instant Pot Ketogenic chilli
Snack	Instant Pot Stuffed olives
Salad	Instant Pot Tuna Salad
Nutrition intake per day:	Calories: 1469.3	Fat: 177.5g	Carbohydrates: 33.7g	Protein 94.8 g	Sugar 9.4g

Breakfast: *Almond flour Bread*

Preview:
Prep Time: 10 min
Cooking Time: 30 min
Total Time: 40 min
Serves: 2
Appliance: Oven

Nutrition per Serving:
Calories: 207.3; Fat: 25g
Carbs: 6.7 g, Protein 7.6g
Sugar: 2.35g

INGREDIENTS

- 1 Cup of almond powder
- 2 tablespoons of coconut flour
- 2 tablespoons of almond butter
- 2 tablespoons of avocado oil
- 1 and 1/2 tablespoons of ghee
- ¼ Tablespoon of baking soda
- 1 Organic egg

Cooking Direction:

1. In a large bowl, mix the almond powder with the coconut flour and the baking soda.
2. Melt the almond butter, the ghee, the avocado oil and add it to the mixture.
3. Add in the egg and mix it very well.
4. Place the dough in a medium bread tray
5. Place the baking tray in the oven and bake it for about 30 minutes 30 at a temperature of about 380° F
6. When the bread is perfectly cooked, set it aside to cool for 5 minutes, then slice it and divide the bread slices between 2 containers.
7. Store the containers in the refrigerator

Storage, freeze, thaw and reheat guideline:
To store your Ketogenic breakfast bread make sure to divide it between 2 containers. Place the containers in the refrigerator at a temperature of about 39 °F. When you want to serve your bread, remove the containers from the refrigerator and set it aside for 15 minutes then microwave it for 5 minutes

Appetizer: *Salmon rolls with cucumber*

Preview:

Prep Time: 5 min
Cooking Time: 5 min
Total Time: 10 min
Serves: 2
Appliance: Oven

Nutrition per Serving:

Calories: 298; Fat: 42g
Carbs: 5.9g, Protein 18.3g
Sugar: 0.1g

Ingredients

- 2 slices of salmon
- 2 small cucumbers
- 1 cup of goat cheese
- ½ lemon
- 2 tablespoons of cream cheese
- 1 cup of grated mozzarella cheese
- Chopped dill
- 1 Pinch of salt
- 1 pinch of pepper
- 1 tablespoon of ghee

Cooking Direction:

1. Wash, peel and cut into small pieces the cucumber.
2. In a bowl, combine the fresh cheese, cream cheese, mozzarella cheese and ghee with cucumber pieces; the juice of half a lemon, the dill, salt and pepper to your liking. Spread the mixture over the whole slice of salmon.
3. Roll the slice, cut the roll horizontally to form small roll
4. Carefully arrange the salmon rolls in two containers
5. Store the containers in the refrigerator

Storage, freeze, thaw and reheat guideline:

To store your appetizer make sure to divide it between 2 containers. Place the containers in the refrigerator at a temperature of about 40 °F. When you want to serve your appetizer, remove the containers from the refrigerator and set it aside

Lunch : *Ketogenic chicken skillet*

Preview :
Prep Time: 8 min
Cooking Time: 15 min
Total Time: 23 min
Serves: 2
Appliance: Oven

Nutrition per Serving:
Calories: 248.2; Fat: 34g
Carbs: 10 g, Protein 21g
Sugar: 3.3g

Ingredients

- 10 oz of boneless chicken breasts
- 2 Tbsp of Worcestershire sauce
- 1/2 tsp of onion powder
- 1/2 tsp of garlic powder
- 1 dash of ground pepper
- 2 tablespoons of avocado oil
- 1 tablespoon of ghee
- 2 tsp of olive oil, divided
- 1/2 cup of fresh diced onion
- 1/2 cup of diced bell pepper
- 1/2 tsp of minced garlic
- 3 slices of provolone cheese
- 1 cup of goat cheese
- 1/2 cup of cream cheese

Cooking Direction:

1. Slice the chicken breasts into thin pieces and place it a medium bowl. Add the next 4 ingredient boneless chicken breasts, the Worcestershire sauce, the onion powder, the garlic powder, avocado oil, goat cheese, cream cheese, ghee with the ground pepper and stir very well to coat the chicken.
2. Heat 1 teaspoon of olive oil in a large oven skillet. Add the chicken pieces and cook it until it is browned for about 5 minutes. Turn the pieces over and cook for about 2 to 3 minutes. Remove from the skillet.
3. Add the remaining 1 teaspoon of olive oil to the warm skillet. Then add the onions, the bell pepper and the garlic. Cook the chicken and stir for about 3 minutes

Storage, freeze, thaw and reheat guideline:

To store your lunch make sure to divide it between 2 containers. Place the containers in the refrigerator at a temperature of about 40 °F. When you want to serve your lunch, remove the containers from the refrigerator and set it aside for 10 minutes then heat it in the

4.	Turn the heat off and add the chicken back to the skillet and stir it with the veggies to combine very well. Place the sliced cheese over the top and cover for about 2 to 3 minutes.	skillet for about 5 minutes
5.	Divide the chicken between two containers; then store it in the refrigerator	

Dinner: *Instant Pot Ketogenic Chili*

Preview:
Prep Time: 5 min
Cooking Time: 30 min
Total Time: 35 min
Serves: 2
Appliance: Instant Pot

Nutrition per Serving:
Calories: 407; Fat: 36.5g
Carbs: 6.1 g, Protein 24.9g
Sugar: 3g

Ingredients

- 1 lb of ground Beef
- 1 lb of ground Sausage
- 1 Medium, chopped green Bell Pepper
- 1/2 Medium, chopped yellow onion
- 1 can of 6 oz of tomato paste
- 2 tablespoons of olive oil
- 1 tablespoon of avocado oil
- 1 Tbsp of chilli Powder
- ½ Tbsp of ground Cumin
- 3 to 4 minced garlic cloves
- 1/3 to ¼ cup of water
- 1 can of 14.05 diced tomatoes in the tomato Juice

Cooking Direction:

1. Preheat your Instant pot by pressing the "Sauté" button
2. Add in the olive oil and avocado oil; then add the ground beef and the sausage to the Instant pot and cook until it becomes brown.
3. Once the meat is browned set the Instant Pot to the function "keep warm/cancel".
4. Add in the rest of the ingredients into your Instant Pot and mix very well.
5. Cover the lid of the instant pot and lock it; then make sure that the steam valve is sealed
6. Select the function Bean/Chilli setting for around 30 minutes
7. Once the chilli is perfectly cooked, the Instant Pot will automatically shift to the function mode "Keep Warm"
8. Let the pressure release naturally or you can rather use the quick release method.
9. Divide the chilli between 2 containers; then top with chopped parsley
10. Store the containers in the refrigerator for 2 days

Storage, freeze, thaw and reheat guideline:

To store your chilli lunch divide it between 2 containers. Place the containers in the refrigerator at a temperature of about 38°F. When you want to serve your lunch, remove the containers from the refrigerator and set it aside for 10 minutes then microwave it for about 4 minutes

Snack : *Instant Pot Stuffed olives*

Preview :
Prep Time: 10 min
Cooking Time: 20 min
Total Time: 30 min
Serves: 2
Appliance: Instant Pot

Nutrition per Serving:
Calories: 156; Fat: 20g
Carbs: 3 g, Protein 13g
Sugar: 1g

Ingredients

- 37 pitted Sicilian green olives
- ¼ lb of ground Italian sausage mild
- ½ cup of almond flour
- ½ tbsp of thyme dried or fresh
- 2 small eggs
- 1 and ½ tbsp of olive oil or avocado oil
- ⅓ cup of sunflower seeds shelled unsalted
- 1 and ½ tbsp of flat leaf parsley
- 2 tsp of garlic powder

Cooking Direction:

- Preheat your Instant pot by pressing the function sauté to about 400° F and grease with 1 and ½ tbsp of oil
- In a food processor, combine all together the almond flour, the sunflower seeds, the parsley, the garlic powder, and the thyme. Process your ingredient until it gets a grainy flour texture. Pour the mixture in a large zippered freezer bag and set it aside.
- Make 2 tiny slits across the middle of each olive opening and try to make that hole wide and set it aside
- With the help of a chopstick or a skewer, stuff each of the olives with the ground sausage
- Beat the egg in a small bowl. Dip the olives in the egg wash, and then put it into a zippered bag

Storage, freeze, thaw and reheat guideline:

To store your stuffed olives, divide it between 2 containers; then place the containers in the refrigerator at a temperature of about 39°F. When you are ready to serve your lunch, remove the containers from the refrigerator and set it aside for about 5 minutes; then

with the coating inside it. Seal the bag and shake it until the olives are coated. • Place the olives in the bottom of the Instant Pot and lock the lid, then seal the valve and set the timer for about 20 minutes at a temperature of about 350° F • Remove the olives from the Instant Pot and divide it between two containers; then store in the refrigerator	microwave it for about 3 minutes

Salad: *Instant Pot Tuna Salad*

Preview:
Prep Time: 5 min
Cooking Time: 30 min
Total Time: 35 min
Serves: 2
Appliance: Instant Pot

Nutrition per Serving:
Calories: 153; Fat: 20 g
Carbs: 2 g, Protein 10g
Sugar: 0.2g

Ingredients

- 1 Pound of fresh tuna
- 1 Cup of coconut milk
- 2 limes
- 2 tablespoons of olive oil
- 1 red pepper
- 1 cup of grated mozzarella cheese
- 1 clove of garlic
- 2 Slices of lemongrass
- 1 tablespoon of olive oil
- 1 pinch of ground pepper
- 1 pinch of salt
- 2 tablespoons of cream cheese

Cooking Direction:

1. Turn on your Instant Pot and press the sauté function; then add in the coconut milk with lemongrass and the garlic and sauté for 10 minutes. Let stand at least 2 hours later
2. Cut the fresh tuna into small cubes. Put them in a dish.
3. Seed the pepper and cut it in small dice. Add them to the tuna.
4. Sprinkle the tuna fish and the peppers with the lime juice, the olive oil and the flavoured coconut milk. Add the mozzarella cheese and cream cheese, then mix very well
5. Sprinkle with 1 pinch of pepper, a little salt, and cover with plastic wrap.
6. Marinate for at least two hours.
7. Divide the salad between 2 containers
8. Store the salad in the refrigerator

Storage, freeze, thaw and reheat guideline:

To store your salad divide it between 2 containers; then place the containers in the refrigerator at a temperature of about 38°F. When you are ready to serve your salad, remove the containers from the refrigerator and set it aside for about 10 minutes

Meal Prep 12

The 26th, 27th and 28th days on keto diet

Meal Prep 12: The 26th, 27th and 28th days on keto diet		
Fresh Food Shopping List for 3 Days	**Meat and fish** 2 Pounds of chicken wings 1 Pound of chicken breast 2 Pounds of beef steak 1 Pound of sugar-free sausage 1 lb of shrimp	**Produce:** Bunch of fresh basil 6 avocados An 8 oz packet of spinach leaves 2 cauliflower heads 1 bunch of celery 5 yellow pepper 2 Pounds of tomatoes Kale chips
	Dairy products: 1 dozen eggs ½ lb of almond butter ½ gallon of unsweetened almond milk 8 oz of grated parmesan cheese 8 oz of packet pepper jack cheese slices 8 oz of Mozzarella cheese Cheddar cheese 8 oz of sour cream	**Frozen products:** 10 oz. packet of frozen broccoli florets 10 oz. packet of frozen spinach sugar-free tomatoes **Flours** 4 cups of almond flour 3 cups Coconut flour **Spices** 2 Heads of garlic Salt Pepper

Breakfast	Egg Cups sith sausage Crumbles
Appetizer	Chicken wings
Lunch	Tandoori Chicken
Lunch	Shrimp Scampi
Snack	Kale chips
Dinner	Steak with Broccoli
Nutrition intake per day:	Calories: 1598.7	Fat: 257g	Carbohydrates: 23.8g	Protein 106.2 g	Sugar 4.2g

Breakfast: *Egg cups with sausage crumbles*	
Preview : Prep Time: 10 min Cooking Time: 10 min Total Time: 20 min Serves: 3 Appliance: Air Fryer	**Nutrition per Serving:** Calories: 189; Fat: 25 g Carbs: 2.1 g, Protein 8g Sugar: 0.5g

Ingredients

- 6 tablespoons of cooked and crumbled sausage
- 6 tablespoons of frozen chopped spinach
- 6 teaspoons of shredded Jack cheese
- ¼ Cup of egg Beaters
- 2 Tablespoons of olive oil

Cooking Direction:	**Storage, freeze, thaw and reheat guideline:**
1. Start the Sausage Crumbles and set it aside 2. Grab the muffin cups and layer about 1 tablespoon of each of the sausage crumbles, the spinach, olive oil and about 1tsp of cheese into the cups. Pour the mixture of the eggs on the top 3. Place the muffin cups into the basket and bake at a temperature of about 330° F for about 10 min. 4. Allow the egg cups to cool for 5 minutes 5. Divide the egg cups between 3 containers and store it in the refrigerator	To store your egg cups, divide it between 3 containers; then place the containers in the refrigerator at a temperature of about 38°F. When you are ready to serve your breakfast, remove the containers from the refrigerator

Appetizer: *Chicken wings*

Preview : Prep Time: 5 min Cooking Time: 20 min Total Time: 25 min Serves: 3 Appliance: Air Fryer	**Nutrition per Serving:** Calories: 359; Fat: 56 g Carbs: 5 g, Protein 35g Sugar: 0.8g

Ingredients

- 15 to 17 whole chicken wings
- 3 tablespoons of seasoning salt
- 2 tablespoons of olive oil
- 1 tbsp of garlic powder
- 1 tbsp of pepper

Cooking Direction:	**Storage, freeze, thaw and reheat guideline:**
1. Mix the spices in a large bowl 2. Rinse the wings into cold water 3. Toss the wings into the mixture of the spices; add olive oil, then toss it with your hand to make sure everything is covered 4. Preheat your air fryer to a temperature of about 370° F for about 4 minutes 5. Place the chicken wings in the basket of the air fryer and cook for about 22 minutes and flip from time to time. 6. Divide the chicken between 3 containers and store it in the refrigerator for 3 days	To store your appetizer, divide the chicken between 3 containers; then place the containers in the refrigerator at a temperature of about 40°F. When you are ready to serve your appetizer, remove the containers from the refrigerator and set it aside for about microwave it

Lunch: *Tandoori Chicken*

Preview :
Prep Time: 20 min
Cooking Time: 35 min
Total Time: 55 min
Serves: 3
Appliance: Air Fryer

Nutrition per Serving:
Calories: 348; Fat: 63 g
Carbs: 5.6 g, Protein 25g
Sugar: 0.5g

Ingredients

- 1 pound of chicken tenders each cut in halves
- ¼ cup of Greek yogurt
- 1 tablespoon of minced ginger
- 1 tablespoon of minced garlic
- ¼ cup of cilantro
- 1 teaspoon of salt
- 2 tablespoons of chopped cilantro for garnishing
- 2 tablespoons of olive oil
- 1 teaspoon of garam masala
- 1 teaspoon of sweet smoked paprika to add a smoky flavor to the meat
- 1 tablespoon of ghee
- 2 teaspoons of lemon juice
- 1 teaspoon of cayenne pepper
- 1 teaspoon of turmeric

Cooking Direction:

1. Mix all the ingredients in a large glass bowl except for the basting oil, the lemon juice and about 2 tablespoons of cilantro and set it aside to marinate for 25 minutes
2. Turn on your Air fryer to a temperature of about 350°F for about 5 minutes.
3. When the time is up, open the air fryer lid and arrange the chicken in the basket of your air fryer and baste the chicken with the ghee; then lock the lid
4. Cook the Tandoori chicken for about 10 minutes
5. Flip the chicken when the time is over and baste the other side; then cook for about 5 minutes
6. Use a meat thermometer and make sure the temperature reaches 320°F

Storage, freeze, thaw and reheat guideline:

To store your Tandoori chicken, divide it between 3 containers; then place the containers in the refrigerator at a temperature of about 38°F. When you are ready to serve your lunch, remove the containers from the

7. Remove the chicken and divide it between 3 containers and add lemons slices and cilantro to each container 8. Store the containers in the refrigerator	refrigerator and set it aside for about microwave it for about4 minutes

Lunch: *Shrimp Scampi*

Preview:
Prep Time: 10 min
Cooking Time: 8 min
Total Time: 18 min
Serves: 3
Appliance: Oven and Air Fryer

Nutrition per Serving:
Calories: 321; Fat: 48 g
Carbs: 3 g, Protein 23g
Sugar: 1g

Ingredients

- 4 tablespoons of almond butter
- 1 tablespoon of lemon juice
- 1 tablespoon of minced garlic
- 2 teaspoons of red pepper flakes
- 2 tablespoons of avocado oil
- 1 tablespoon of chopped chives
- 1 tablespoon of minced basil leaves
- 2 tablespoons of chicken stock
- 1 lb of defrosted shrimp

Cooking Direction:

1. Turn your air fryer to a temperature of 330°F. Then place a metal pan of 6 x 3 in the oven
2. Put the almond butter, avocado oil, the garlic and the red pepper flakes in the hot pan
3. Cook for about 2 minutes and stir until the butter is melted
4. Open your air fryer, add all your ingredients to the pan and stir
5. Cook the shrimp for about 5 minutes, and stir
6. Remove the pan with the help of silicone mitts and set aside for 1 minute; then stir again
7. Divide the shrimp between 3 containers and top with fresh chopped basil leaves
8. Store in the refrigerator

Storage, freeze, thaw and reheat guideline:

To store your shrimp scampi, divide it between 3 containers; then place the containers in the refrigerator at a temperature of about 40°F. When you are ready to serve your lunch, remove the containers from the refrigerator and microwave it for about 5 minutes

Snack : *Instant Pot Kale Chips*

Preview : Prep Time: 10 min Cooking Time: 8 min Total Time: 18 min Serves: 3 Appliance: Instant Pot	**Nutrition per Serving:** Calories: 136.3; Fat: 27.4 g Carbs: 3.6 g, Protein 4.5g Sugar: 1.4g

Ingredients

- 1 large bunch of kale
- 2 Tablespoons of Avocado oil
- 1 pinch of Chilli powder
- 1 Pinch of salt
- 1 Pinch of pepper

Cooking Direction:

1. Preheat your Instant Pot to a temperature of 360° F by pressing the setting function sauté
2. Rip the kale into tiny pieces and remove any hard spines from it
3. Add the kale to the Instant pot; then spray it with oil and coat very well
4. Add the chilli powder, the salt and the pepper.
5. Sauté the kale for about 5 minutes
6. Add the kale to a plate and season it with chilli powder
7. Divide the kale chips between 3 containers and store it in the refrigerator.

Storage, freeze, thaw and reheat guideline:

To store your kale kale chips, divide it between 3 containers; then place the containers in the refrigerator at a temperature of about 38°F. When you are ready to serve your snack, remove the containers from the refrigerator and microwave it for about 3 minutes

Dinner : *Steak with broccoli*

Preview :
Prep Time: 5 min
Cooking Time: 5 min
Total Time: 10 min
Serves: 3
Appliance: Instant Pot

Nutrition per Serving:
Calories: 245.4; Fat: 37.6g
Carbs: 4.5 g, Protein 10.7g
Sugar: 2.3g

Ingredients

- 1/2 small thinly sliced red onion
- 3 tbsp of red wine vinegar
- 1 pinch of kosher salt
- 1 Pinch of freshly ground black pepper
- 5 tbsp of divided extra-virgin olive oil
- 1 and 1/4 lb of cut skirt steak
- 1 tsp of ground coriander
- 1 thinly sliced small head of broccoli
- 4 c. of mâche
- 1/4 Cup of roasted sunflower seeds
- 4 oz, 1/4 cup of shaved ricotta

Cooking Direction:

8. Combine the vinegar, and about 1/2 teaspoon of salt in a bowl. Then set it aside
9. Meanwhile, press the function sauté of your Instant pot and heat about 1 tablespoon in it; then season the steak with the coriander, the salt, and the pepper.
10. Lock the lid of your Instant Pot
11. Cook for about 5 minutes at a temperature of 365°F
12. Add the broccoli, the mâche, the sunflower seeds, and the remaining 4 tablespoons oil to the onions and toss to combine it.
13. Season the steak with 1 pinch of salt and the pepper.

Storage, freeze, thaw and reheat guideline:

To store your dinner, divide it between 3 containers; then put the containers in the refrigerator at a temperature of about 40°F. When you are ready to serve your dinner, remove the containers from the refrigerator and microwave it for about 4 minutes

Conclusion

Eat healthy, gain more energy and lose weight is always my dream and the dream of any person. And for this reason, I am passionate about my health and getting the weight loss. I thought of offering you this Keto Meal Prep cookbook. Thus, I wrote this book to share my experience with you and to help everyone who feels they can't lose weight. And to save your time and help you organize your meals with meal prep.

Firstly, I want to tell you that you must never lose hope, no matter how much you weight, and no matter how hard it can be. You should believe in yourself because you can do it. When I started the meal prep Keto recipes, I thought I would never succeed, but after a few days, I got used to it and I noticed an important progress in losing weight.

The recipes in this book, which are all inspired by my personal experience; will help you through your journey of losing weight in your daily life. I have created a wide range of meal prep recipes that will suit everyone's budget and agenda. By reading this Meal Prep cookbook, you will never have to worry about your extra pounds. Try the Keto Meal Prep recipes in order to lose weight fast and to become healthy.

We really hope you enjoyed this book. If you found this material helpful feel free to share it with friends. You can also help others find it by leaving a review where you purchased the book. Your feedback will help us continue to write books you love.

Make sure and check out the other wonderful books in our catalog and of course to buy our Keto diet book for a much more healthy life!

We would love to hear how the results were.

Made in the USA
Middletown, DE
13 August 2018